PRAISE FOR *A STRANGE LOOP*

"Subversive, polymorphous genius . . . Identity crisis is the engine that drives this dense, whirling gyre of code-switching satire and metatheatrical self-discovery to dazzling effect."

—DAVID COTE, *OBSERVER*

"One of the most original and exciting works of the past twenty years."

—ELYSA GARDNER, *NEW YORK STAGE REVIEW*

"Rich with clever comedy and eviscerating honesty . . . Michael R. Jackson's heady metamusical starts strong and goes to lots of strong places . . . By diving into the excruciatingly personal, he finds the broadly human."

—SARA HOLDREN, *NEW YORK*

"One hundred uninterrupted minutes of the rawest, funniest, most uncomfortably honest musical you're likely to see all year."

—ZACHARY STEWART, *THEATERMANIA*

"Exhilarating . . . *A Strange Loop* is bolstered by vibrant songs and cutting lyrics . . . The abundantly talented Jackson takes the otherwise tired trope of the young, poor, and sensitive artist trying to discover his true self and make it in New York, then adds layer upon layer of personal angst from a fresh and startling perspective. Offers bracing insights into the endless strata of conflicts faced by those who are young, gifted, and Black—and so much more."

—FRANK RIZZO, *VARIETY*

"Genuinely breathtaking because it forces you to gasp before you break out laughing . . . Jackson wrote the music, lyrics, *and* the book for *A Strange Loop*. Usually, that three-hat trick in the musical theater world is the mark of death. Jackson wears all hats with fabulous style."

—ROBERT HOFLER, *WRAP*

"While *A Strange Loop* is clever and funny, it is also very raw and not for the faint of heart. Jackson pulls no punches in his language or his exploration of [the character] Usher's experiences."

—DONNA HERMAN, *NEW YORK THEATRE GUIDE*

"A clever, tuneful, and gloriously neurotic mix of self-exploration and social commentary, *A Strange Loop* features bouncy and energetic theater-pop melodies propelling lyrics infused with wittily expressed angst . . . Sharp and funny."

—MICHAEL DALE, *BROADWAY WORLD*

"Michael R. Jackson's semi-autobiographical *A Strange Loop* transforms oversharing into high art . . . A score that's fresh, unpredictable, and inextricably blended with the book and lyrics . . . An intriguing odyssey with plenty of momentum, fresh melodies, and artful lyrics that explore essential elements of the human condition."

—CHARLES WRIGHT, *CURTAINUP*

"Jackson is an undisputedly talented and promising young artist . . . Inventive touches and songs full of both spark and sensitivity."

—MATT WINDMAN, *AMNY*

A STRANGE LOOP

A STRANGE LOOP

BOOK, MUSIC, AND LYRICS BY

Michael R. Jackson

THEATRE COMMUNICATIONS GROUP / NEW YORK / 2020

A Strange Loop is published by Theatre Communications Group, Inc.,
520 Eighth Avenue, 24th Floor, New York, NY 10018-4156

The publication of *A Strange Loop* by Michael R. Jackson, through TCG's Book Program, is made possible in part by the New York State Council on the Arts with the support of Governor Andrew Cuomo and the New York State Legislature.

Special thanks to the board and staff of Playwrights Horizons for their generous support of this publication, in recognition of outgoing Artistic Director Tim Sanford.

TCG books are exclusively distributed to the book trade by Consortium Book Sales and Distribution.

Library of Congress Control Numbers:
2020035401 (print) / 2020035402 (ebook)
ISBN 978-1-55936-993-0 (paperback) / ISBN 978-1-55936-994-7 (ebook)
A catalog record for this book is available from the Library of Congress.

Book design and composition by Lisa Govan
Cover design by Jeff Rogers

First Edition, November 2020
Third Printing, January 2023

A Strange Loop is dedicated to Darius Marcel Smith
and "all those Black gay boys I knew
who chose to go on back to the Lord . . ."

DARIUS MARCEL SMITH
(SEPTEMBER 13, 1982–FEBRUARY 25, 2019)

A STRANGE LOOP

A Strange Loop received its world premiere at Playwrights Horizons (Tim Sanford, Artistic Director; Leslie Marcus, Managing Director; Carol Fishman, General Manager) in New York, in association with Page 73 (Michael Walkup, Artistic Director; Amanda Feldman, Managing Director), on June 17, 2019. It was originally developed at Musical Theatre Factory (Shakina Nayfack, Founding Artistic Director). It was directed by Stephen Brackett. It was choreographed by Raja Feather Kelly. The scenic design was by Arnulfo Maldonado, the costume design was by Montana Levi Blanco, the lighting design was by Jen Schriever, the sound design was by Alex Hawthorn, and the orchestrations were by Charlie Rosen; the musical director was Rona Siddiqui and the production stage manager was Erin Gioia Albrecht. The cast was:

USHER	Larry Owens
THOUGHT 1	L Morgan Lee
THOUGHT 2	James Jackson, Jr.
THOUGHT 3	John-Michael Lyles
THOUGHT 4	John-Andrew Morrison
THOUGHT 5	Jason Veasey
THOUGHT 6	Antwayn Hopper

SETTING

A loop within a loop within a loop inside a perception of one man's reality.

CHARACTERS

Usher: A fat American Black gay man of high intelligence, low self-image, and deep feelings. He writes stories and songs and wants desperately to be heard. A musical theater writer and Broadway usher.

Thoughts 1–6: A spectrum of bodies that are Usher's perceptions of reality inside and out. They come in many shapes and sizes. But they are all Black. And they are as individual in expression as they are a unit.

SONGS

The fire you like so much in me
is the mark of someone adamantly free . . .

—LIZ PHAIR, "STRANGE LOOP"

Blackness. Intermission chimes. Lights on Usher with his back to us, ringing chimes from the back of a theater, which manifests as a strange loop in his mind, along with silhouettes of his Thoughts.

INTERMISSION SONG (INTRO)

ALL THOUGHTS:
>USHER-USHER! USHER! USHER!
>USHER-USHER! USHER! USHER!
>USHER-USHER! USHER! USHER!
>USHER-USHER! USHER! USHER! . . .

(Usher turns around, chiming.)

USHER: Ladies and gentlemen, please return to your seats; the second act is about to begin! Ladies and gentlemen, please return to your seats; the second act is about to begin! There will be performers running down the aisles and wearing pantaloons and gaudy flowing robes that I think are meant to indicate the wholesome beauty of "Mother Africa"! There will be swinging birds on fishing poles and a Black Ken doll with a crossover dialect in a lion costume! What else? Oh, yes! In the background, there will be a young overweight-to-obese homosexual and/or gay and/or queer, cisgender male, able-bodied university-and-graduate-school-educated, musical-theater-writing, Disney-ushering, broke-ass middle-class far-Left-leaning Black-identified-and-classified American descendant of slaves full of self-conscious femme energy and who thinks he's probably a vers bottom but not totally certain of that, obsessing over the latest draft of his self-referential musical *A Strange Loop*! And surrounded by his *extremely* obnoxious Thoughts!

USHER:	ALL THOUGHTS:
A STRANGE LOOP WILL HAVE BLACK SHIT! AND WHITE SHIT! HE'LL GIVE YOU UPTOWN AND DOWNTOWN! WITH CODE-SWITCHING AND BUTT-FUCKING! THERE *WILL* BE BUTT-FUCKING! SO PLEASE RETURN TO YOUR SEATS BECAUSE—but can I really write this?	USHER-USHER! USHER! USHER! USHER-USHER! USHER! USHER! USHER-USHER! USHER USHER! USHER-USHER! USHER! USHER! . . .

(OPENING) INTERMISSION SONG

THOUGHT 1:
    HOW MANY MINUTES 'TIL THE
    END OF INTERMISSION?

THOUGHT 2:

IS THAT HOW THE SHOW SHOULD OPEN?

THOUGHT 1:

SHOULD THERE EVEN BE A SHOW?

THOUGHT 2:

NO, IT SHOULD START WITH WHAT HE'S THINKING

THOUGHT 1:

WHICH IS JUST A CURSOR BLINKING

THOUGHTS 1 AND 2:

'CAUSE OF ALL OF THE DIRECTIONS
THAT THE NARRATIVE COULD GO!

USHER:

HE WANTS TO SHOW WHAT
IT'S LIKE TO LIVE UP HERE
AND TRAVEL THE WORLD IN A
FAT, BLACK QUEER BODY

THOUGHTS 1 AND 2:

OH USHER . . .

THOUGHTS 5 AND 6:

HOW MANY MINUTES 'TIL THE
END OF INTERMISSION?
NO ONE CARES ABOUT A WRITER WHO IS
STRUGGLING TO WRITE

THOUGHT 4:

THEY'LL SAY IT'S WAY TOO REPETITIOUS

THOUGHT 3:

AND SO OVERLY AMBITIOUS

THOUGHTS 5 AND 6:

    WHICH OF COURSE MAKES THEM SUSPICIOUS

THOUGHTS 3 AND 6:

    THAT YOU THINK YOU'RE FUCKING WHITE!

USHER:

HE HAS TO FIGHT FOR HIS   THOUGHTS 3–6:

RIGHT TO LIVE IN A WORLD   HEY, USHER . . .

THAT CHEWS UP AND SPITS

OUT BLACK QUEERS

ON THE DAILY

THOUGHTS 1 AND 2:

    BLACKNESS, QUEERNESS FIGHTING BACK TO

        FILL THIS CIS-HET-ALL-WHITE SPACE WITH A—

THOUGHTS 3 AND 4:

    PORTRAIT OF A PORTRAIT OF A PORTRAIT OF A

        BLACK QUEER FACE

THOUGHTS 1–4:

    AND A CHOIR FULL OF BLACK QUEER VOICES,

        TREBLE CLEF

THOUGHTS 5 AND 6:

    AND ALSO BASS

ALL THOUGHTS:

    THAT ARE CASTING SPELLS TO CONJURE UP A

USHER:

    BIG, BLACK AND QUEER-ASS

    AMERICAN BROADWAY—

THOUGHTS 4–6:
BIG, BLACK AND QUEER-ASS
AMERICAN BROADWAY—

USHER AND ALL THOUGHTS:
BIG, BLACK AND QUEER-ASS
AMERICAN BROADWAY SHOW!

(Dance Break: Usher and the Thoughts put on a Big, Black and Queer-Ass American Broadway Show.)

ALL THOUGHTS:
HOW MANY MINUTES 'TIL THE
END OF INTERMISSION?

THOUGHTS 1 AND 4:
'TIL HE HAS TO FACE THE FACT THAT
HE IS REALLY IN A JAM

THOUGHTS 5 AND 6:
HE HAS NO PATRONS HE CAN CALL ON
NOR A BACKUP PLAN TO FALL ON

THOUGHTS 2 AND 3:
JUST A HAMSTER WHEEL TO CRAWL ON

THOUGHTS 1 AND 5:
AND NOBODY GIVES A DAMN!

USHER, THOUGHTS 2 AND 6:
HE TRIES TO SCRAMBLE AND
DODGE OR EXTRICATE STILL
HIS FATE LIES IN WAIT LIKE A
SCAVENGING VULTURE

THOUGHTS 3 AND 4:
HEY, USHER . . .

USHER AND THOUGHT 3:
ALL HE WANTS IS TO SUBVERT
EXPECTATIONS BLACK AND
WHITE FROM THE LEFT AND
THE RIGHT FOR THE GOOD OF
THE CULTURE

THOUGHTS 1–2, 4–6:
OH, USHER . . .

THOUGHT 6:
OH, USHER . . .

ALL THOUGHTS:
USHER-USHER! USHER! USHER!
USHER-USHER! USHER! USHER!
HOW MANY MINUTES 'TIL THE
END OF INTERMISSION?
YOU'RE A BALL OF BLACK CONFUSION THAT
KEEPS HITTING A PLATEAU

THOUGHT 2:
YOU CAN'T JUST FLOUT EVERY CONVENTION

THOUGHT 3:
THEN COMMAND COMPLETE ATTENTION IN A

USHER:
BIG, BLACK AND QUEER-ASS
AMERICAN BROADWAY SHOW!

THOUGHTS 4–6:
HOW MANY MINUTES 'TIL THE
END OF INTERMISSION?
SOME SAY WRITE FROM EXPLORATION
SOME SAY JUST WRITE WHAT YOU KNOW

THOUGHT 5:
BUT EITHER WAY YOU KEEP CAREENING SO IT'S
HARD TO FIND THE MEANING IN YOUR—

USHER:

> BIG, BLACK AND QUEER-ASS
> AMERICAN BROADWAY SHOW!

ALL THOUGHTS:

> HOW MANY MINUTES 'TIL THE
> END OF INTERMISSION?
> IF YOU CAN'T PLEASE THE CAUCASIANS
> YOU WILL NEVER GET THE DOUGH—

THOUGHTS 1 AND 2:

> PLUS CRITICS CLINICALLY DENY US
> THEN DENY IMPLICIT BIAS

THOUGHTS 5 AND 6:

> WITH THEIR VANITY SUPPORTED
> BY A SYSTEM THAT'S DISTORTED

THOUGHT 4:

> WATCH THEM WRITE YOU OFF AS LAZY
> NOT TO MENTION NAVEL-GAZY

ALL THOUGHTS:

> LACKING BOTH IN CRAFT AND RIGOR

THOUGHT 3:

> 'CAUSE YOU'RE JUST
> A FUCKING [NIG]—

THOUGHTS 1–2, 4–6:

> BIG, BLACK AND QUEER-ASS
> AMERICAN BROADWAY—
> BIG, BLACK AND QUEER-ASS
> AMERICAN BROADWAY—

ALL THOUGHTS:

> BIG, BLACK AND QUEER-ASS
> AMERICAN BROADWAY—

ALL THOUGHTS:

USHER-USHER! USHER! USHER!

USHER-USHER! USHER! USHER!   USHER:

USHER-USHER! USHER! USHER! . . .   OH MY GOD

OH MY GOD

HOW MANY MINUTES 'TIL THE   OH MY GOD . . .

END OF INTERMISSION? . . .   LESS THAN TWO!!!

THOUGHT 5: Okay, so what's the tea, bitch?

USHER: Ummmmm . . .

THOUGHT 2: Where's the sweat, Usher; you're not even trying!

THOUGHT 6: What's next, what's next?

USHER: I don't know—

THOUGHT 4: Well, you better figure it out!

THOUGHT 1: And fast!

TODAY

USHER: Okay, okay, I got this, I got this. I think after intermission, Usher should get an early dismissal by his shift supervisor so he can go home to work on *A Strange Loop*.

THOUGHT 3: Let's get into it, honey!

(Usher exits into a locker room and begins to change clothes.)

USHER:

> I AM A DISNEY USHER
> I'M BARELY SCRAPING BY
> MY DISCONTENTMENT COMES IN

MANY SHAPES AND SIZES
BUT I WOKE UP THIS MORNING
I TOLD MYSELF TO TRY
I TOLD MYSELF THAT I WOULD
MAKE NO COMPROMISES. TODAY . . .

A MEETING WITH MY LANDLORD
WHO MAKES ME MISS MY TRAIN
AND I SMELL AWFUL
'CAUSE THERE IS NO TIME TO SHOWER
I PLASTER ON A SMILE
PRETEND I HAVE NO BRAIN
MAKE NICE WITH ASSHOLE TOURISTS.
HOUR AFTER HOUR TODAY . . .
TODAY I PLAN TO CHANGE MY WHOLE LIFE
    FOREVER . . .

THOUGHT 2: USHER! SURPRISE!
    (*À la Wendy Williams*) How U doin'? IT'S YOUR
DAILY SELF-LOATHING! And I had some time to kill
so I thought I'd drop in to remind you of just how truly
worthless you are.

THOUGHT 6: Hey, Usher!
    (*À la Wendy Williams*) How U doin'? It's your Finan-
cial Faggotry and ooh chile, do you have a second to chat
about this situation with *Shittybank Student Loans*?

USHER:
    REWRITE THAT SHITTY LYRIC
    TO MAKE THE ENDING LAND
    CONDENSE THE REPETITION
    TO ITS MOST ESSENTIAL
    DEFINE A FORMAL STRUCTURE

SO PEOPLE UNDERSTAND
PULL OUT THE STOPS TO SHOW HIS STORY'S
    FULL POTENTIAL TODAY . . .
TODAY I PLAN TO CHANGE THIS SHOW FOR THE
    BETTER . . .

THOUGHT 5: Usher! Hi, babe! I'm with Corporate Niggatry! Just checking in to see if you were ready to invest in the Beyhive, the Stellar Awards, or Wakanda Forever so we can finally get you into *something* unapologetically Black?

THOUGHT 1: Usher! As supervisor of your sexual ambivalence, you can rest assured that I have sealed the gates of your body and mind so that nothing can get inside your shitty butthole until *you* give the word!

USHER:

I WANT TO BREAK THE CYCLE
THAT'S SO INGRAINED IN ME
BUT CHANGE COMES WAY TOO SLOW
AND I AM IN A HURRY
THERE'S ALL OF THIS REJECTION
WHICH BRINGS SUCH MISERY
BUT WITH MY WHITE GIRL MUSIC
I DROWN OUT THE FLURRY OF TODAY . . .

I AM A DISNEY USHER
I'M BARELY SCRAPING BY
MY DISCONTENTMENT COMES IN
MANY SHAPES AND SIZES
WHEN I WAKE UP EACH MORNING
I TELL MYSELF TO TRY
I TELL MYSELF THAT I WILL
MAKE NO COMPROMISES

SO DAYS LIKE THIS JUST GET ME
I HATE DAYS LIKE TODAY
DAYS WHEN I SEE MYSELF AND
SEE THE SAME REFLECTION
SOMEONE WHO'S STUCK REWRITING
BUT STUCK IN HIS OWN WAY
SOMEONE WHO PLANS TO EDIT
EVERY IMPERFECTION. TODAY.
TODAY I PLAN TO CHANGE MY SELF—

THOUGHT 2: Oh, girl, *whatever*!

USHER: Okay. So the work day is done, he's about to sit down to write which is of course the precise moment he gets a call from—

(Each Thought eats from a Popeyes box as Usher writes.)

THOUGHT 4: USHERRRRRRRR!!!!!!!!!!!! IT'S YOUR *MOTHER* CALLIIIIIIIING!!!!!

THOUGHT 3: I ain't want nuthin'.

THOUGHT 5: I just thought you might be interested to know about some more of this mess goin' on with yo' brutha, yo' niece, and her *airheaded mama*—

THOUGHT 6: who been goin' around tellin' different people at church like that dat-blasted airheaded Marion that God sent her a vision of you touchin' Nala—

THOUGHT 1: *on* the vagina—

THOUGHT 2: at the family reunion las' July.

THOUGHT 5: Now I'unno if Nala even know what a vagina *is* or not—

THOUGHT 1: let alone whether somebody done *touched* her on it—

THOUGHT 3: but since she don't know no better than to repeat after her *airheaded mama*—

THOUGHT 4: now Nala goin' aroun' tellin' different people at church like that dat-blasted airheaded Marion that you "touched" her—

THOUGHT 5: *on* the vagina—

THOUGHT 2: at the family reunion las' July—

THOUGHT 6: so now *Rafficki*—

THOUGHT 3: yo' niece's *"mother"*—

THOUGHT 1: "doesn't know if she feel comfortable letting her dorter come over to her grandmother and grandfather house—"

THOUGHT 5: "not if we just gonna be lettin' her get *molested all the time.*"

THOUGHT 2: Now how you like them apples?

THOUGHT 1: *That's why I cain't lose no weight.*

THOUGHT 4: 'Cause I be gettin' into it wit' different people and get to feeling so melancholy that all I can do is sit here with this *dat-blasted* Popeyes when *IT AIN'T EVEN GOOD!*

WE WANNA KNOW

THOUGHT 2: But annnnnnnnnnyway . . . that's not why I called.

THOUGHT 3: I called 'cause I wanna discuss my son!

THOUGHT 5: Are you still flowing within your purpose and lettin' the Lord lead ya and guide ya and direct thy path?

THOUGHT 6: Are you still urshering?

THOUGHT 1: When you gon' get discovered?

THOUGHT 3: Ain't it about time for a producer to give you the hook up on one of yo' musical the-A-ter writings?

THOUGHT 4: And what about yo' friend Toya? She still married to that guy? You think she might ever change her mind and get sweet on you? C'mon, Son! What's the 4-1-1?

ALL THOUGHTS:
    WE WANNA KNOW
    WHAT'S GOIN' ON IN NEW YORK
    WE WANNA KNOW
    WHAT'S GOIN' ON IN YA LIFE
    WIT' PEOPLE THERE LIVING ANY WHICH-A WAY
    AND TO HECK WITH WHAT THE B-I-B-L-E SAY

    WE WANNA KNOW
    WHAT'S GOIN' ON IN NEW YORK
    WE WANNA KNOW
    IF YOU BEEN CHASING YA DREAM
    'CAUSE AFTER WHAT ME AND YO' DAD WENT
        THROUGH
    TO SEND YO' BLACK BOOTIE TO NYU

    IT APPEARS YOU BE JES' RUNNING AROUND
    AND WITHOUT ANY DIRECTION

THOUGHT 2:
    AND WITHOUT ANY DIRECTION

THOUGHT 1:
    AND WITHOUT ANY DIRECTION

THOUGHTS 3–6:
    IF THAT'S WHAT YOU REALLY WANTED TO DO
    THEN WHY AIN'T YOU JUST STAY HERE?

THOUGHT 1: 'Cause you selfish.

ALL THOUGHTS:
    EVERY TIME WE CALL YOU UP YOU JUST CLAIM
    THAT YOU DONE MADE SOME CONNECTION

THOUGHT 2: You so full o' doo-doo, yo' eyes is brown.

ALL THOUGHTS:

> YOU CAN LIE TO YOURSELF IF YOU WANT
> BUT YOU CAIN'T LIE TO ME, DEAR

THOUGHT 4: You say you be off writin' musicals but what the heck kinda music you be writin'?

THOUGHT 1: It probably sound like that dat-blasted white girl music you used to listen to 'n' try to hide from me 'n' y' dad when you was in high school, don't it?

THOUGHT 2: You ain't up there in New York thinking you a white girl wit' yo' musical the-A-ter writings is you?

THOUGHT 5: 'Cause every time we ask, you just say you be writin' "about 'life'"!

THOUGHT 3: And I'm like *LIFE*! What you know about *life*?

THOUGHT 6: You ain't but twenty-five years old!

THOUGHT 3: Almost *twenty-six*!

THOUGHT 2: You gon' turn twenty-six *on* the twenty-six.

THOUGHT 4: But I'on care if you twenty-six or a *hundred* and twenty-six, I did all the work to birf you in this world so now *it's time for you to give back.* I gotta *job* for you:

ALL THOUGHTS:

> YOU RUNNING AROUN' THERE WIT' A MFA
> SO NOW YOU GONNA WRITE ME A GOSPEL PLAY.

THOUGHT 4: Like *Tyler Perry*.

THOUGHT 5: 'Cause *Tyler Perry* writes real life.

THOUGHT 3: *Tyler Perry* knows how to bring everything together wit' all the *stories*? And all the *singing*? And all the different people *talking*?

THOUGHT 1: And *Tyler Perry* don't never forget to bring in the spirit'ch'alities.

THOUGHT 2: 'Cause *Tyler Perry* loves his mama—

THOUGHT 6: And the Lord—

THOUGHT 1: So write a nice, clean Tyler Perry–like gospel play for your parents please—

THOUGHT 5: It's the *least* your Black butt can do after all the love we done gave—

THOUGHT 6: And all the money we done come off of—

THOUGHT 3: Unless you just don't love your mama—

THOUGHT 4: Or the Lord . . .

INNER WHITE GIRL

USHER:

ON DAYS HIS BLACKNESS FEELS LIKE ANOTHER
   HURDLE
THAT WON'T GET OUT OF HIS WAY
HIS INNER WHITE GIRL STARTS KICKING LIKE
   A BABY
SHE WANTS TO COME OUT AND PLAY
SHE DOESN'T CARE IF SHE RUFFLES ANY FEATHERS
IN FACT, THAT IS HER M.O.
WHERE HE'S THE KING OF AVOIDING
   CONFRONTATION
THERE'S NOT A BOMB SHE WON'T THROW BECAUSE

USHER AND ALL THOUGHTS:

WHITE GIRLS CAN DO ANYTHING, CAN'T THEY?
BLACK BOYS MUST ALWAYS OBEY THEIR MOTHERS!
WHITE GIRLS CAN DO ANYTHING, CAN'T THEY?
CAN'T THEY? CAN'T THEY? CAN'T THEY?

USHER:
SOME DAYS HE FEELS
   LIKE HIS BLACKNESS
IS A TREASURE
THAT'S UNDER
   CONSTANT ATTACK
HIS INNER WHITE GIRL
   PROTECTS IT
FROM MARAUDERS
SHE ALWAYS TAKES
   UP THE SLACK
SHE LETS HIM FEEL LIKE
   A HUMAN SUPERNOVA
LIKE HE COULD
   CONQUER THE EARTH
LIKE HE'S THE HEIR
   TO THE POWER
   AND OPPRESSION
HER KIND HAVE
   WIELDED SINCE
   BIRTH

BECAUSE

THOUGHTS 1 AND 3:
WHO, WHO IS YOU?
WHO, WHO IS YOU?

THOUGHTS 5 AND 6:
HEH, HEH, HEH, HEH,
   HEH, HEH,
   HEH . . .

THOUGHTS 1 AND 3:
WHO, WHO IS YOU?
WHO, WHO IS YOU?

THOUGHTS 2 AND 4:
HEH, HEH, HEH, HEH,
   HEH, HEH,
   HEH . . .

ALL THOUGHTS:
WHO . . . WHO . . . WHO . . . ?
BECAUSE . . .

USHER AND ALL THOUGHTS:
   WHITE GIRLS CAN DO ANYTHING, CAN'T THEY?
   BLACK BOYS MUST ALWAYS OBEY THEIR MOTHERS!
   WHITE GIRLS CAN DO ANYTHING, CAN'T THEY?
   CAN'T THEY? CAN'T THEY? CAN'T THEY?

USHER:
THEY GET TO BE "COOL,
   TALL, VULNERABLE
   AND LUSCIOUS . . ."

ALL THOUGHTS:
DO, DO, DO, DO, DO, DO,
   DO, DO, DO, DO

USHER *(Continued)*:
THEY GET TO BE
   WILD AND UNWISE
THEY GET TO BE
   SHY AND
   INTROSPECTIVE
THEY GET TO
   MAKE NOISE
THEY GET TO
   MESMERIZE
BLACK BOYS
DON'T GET TO BE
   "COOL, TALL,
   VULNERABLE AND
   LUSCIOUS . . ."
DON'T GET TO BE
   WILD AND UNWISE
DON'T GET TO BE
   SHY AND
   INTROSPECTIVE
DON'T GET TO
   MAKE NOISE
DON'T GET TO
   FANTASIZE . . .

ALL THOUGHTS *(Continued)*:
DO, DO, DO, DO, DO, DO,
   DO, DO, DO, DO

DO, DO, DO, DO, DO, DO,
   DO, DO, DO, DO

DO, DO, DO, DO, DO, DO,
   DO, DO, DO, DO

DO, DO, DO, DO, DO, DO,
   DO, DO, DO, DO

DO, DO, DO, DO, DO, DO,
   DO, DO, DO, DO
DO, DO, DO, DO, DO, DO,
   DO, DO, DO, DO

DO, DO, DO, DO, DO,
   DO, DO, DO, DO,
OOH . . . AH . . .

USHER:
   HIS BLACKNESS DOESN'T LOOK BLUE IN ANY
      MOONLIGHT
   WHICH MAKES HIM HARDER TO SEE
   THAT'S WHY HE CLINGS TO HIS SILLY INNER
      WHITE GIRL
   THE SAME ONE CLINGING TO ME

USHER:	ALL THOUGHTS:
WE WANT TO BE FREE	OOH . . .
WE WANT TO BELONG	OOH . . .
WE WANT EITHER LOVE	OOH . . . LOVE . . .
OR VALIDATION	
BUT NEITHER COME	OOH . . .
EASILY	OOH . . .
SO HER SIREN SONG	
KEEPS US IN TOTAL	OOH . . .
SUBJUGATION . . .	

THOUGHTS 1 AND 2:
TOTAL SUBJUGATION . . .

USHER:	THOUGHTS 1–4:
WE WANT TO BE "COOL,	WHITE GIRLS CAN DO
TALL, VULNERABLE	ANYTHING, CAN'T THEY?
AND LUSCIOUS . . ."	BLACK BOYS MUST ALWAYS
	OBEY THEIR MOTHERS!

	THOUGHTS 5 AND 6:
WE WANT TO BE	HEH, HEH, HEH, HEH,
WILD AND UNWISE	HEH, HEH, HEH . . .
	AND BLACK!
	AND BLACK!

	THOUGHTS 3 AND 4:
WE WANT TO BE	WHITE GIRLS CAN DO
SHY AND	ANYTHING, CAN'T THEY?
INTROSPECTIVE	CAN'T THEY? CAN'T THEY?
	CAN'T THEY?

	THOUGHTS 1 AND 2 *(On loop)*:
WE WANT TO	WHO, WHO, IS YOU?
MAKE NOISE	WHO, WHO IS YOU? . . .

USHER *(Continued)*:
WE WANT TO   THOUGHTS 5 AND 6:
    MESMERIZE   HEH, HEH, HEH, HEH,
                             HEH, HEH, HEH . . .
                         BE BLACK! BE BLACK!

                         THOUGHTS 3 AND 4:
WHY CAN'T WE BE "COOL,   WHITE GIRLS CAN DO
    TALL, VULNERABLE   ANYTHING, CAN'T THEY?
    AND LUSCIOUS"?   BLACK BOYS MUST ALWAYS
                             OBEY THEIR MOTHERS!

                         THOUGHTS 5 AND 6:
WHY CAN'T WE EXPRESS   WHITE GIRLS CAN DO
    IN OUR OWN WAY?   ANYTHING, CAN'T THEY?
                         YOU BLACK! YOU BLACK!

USHER:
    WHY CAN'T WE UNLEASH WHAT'S LOCKED INSIDE
    US?
    WHO MADE UP THESE RULES THAT BLACK BOYS
    HAVE TO OBEY?

(The Thoughts each peruse a draft of A Strange Loop *critically.)*

THOUGHT 3: Uh-huh. And an inner white girl is who or what
    exactly?
USHER: Like Liz Phair? Tori Amos? Joni Mitchell? People like
    that? It's really more of an abstract concept than anything
    I think.
THOUGHT 3: Oy. And just so I'm understanding correctly, he
    just turns his back to us? That's seriously how the show
    ends?

USHER: Possibly. In this draft at least.

THOUGHT 3: Hmm. Well, that's certainly a choice.

THOUGHT 5: I just wish the protagonist of *A Strange Loop* were someone I could imagine shagging because whether it's the *Me Too* era or not, fuckability is still the lifeblood of the theater, darling. There shouldn't be a limp dick or a dry pussy in the house when your lead takes his clothes off.

THOUGHT 2: Okay, I'm sorry but you can't say "n" in a musical. I'm sorry. You can't say it *ever* actually. I'm sorry. White people are watching. I'm sorry. Black people are watching. I'm sorry. Don't roll your eyes at me; I'm the chair of the Second-Coming-of-Sondheim Award so I know what the fuck I'm talking about!

THOUGHT 4: Every time you present to our Guardians of Musical Theatre Centrism Tribunal, I find myself longing for the days when musicals were *quieter* and more centered around the lives and concerns of civilized, property-owning adults.

THOUGHT 6: Yeah, I mean, why not make it be about slavery or police violence so the allies in your audience have something *intersectional* to hold on to? I mean, not to give away a trade secret, but I bought two of my houses on slavery, police violence and intersectionality, my brutha.

USHER: I hadn't thought of that. Intersectionality is so amazing. Absolutely.

THOUGHT 1: Well, I like your piece. I think the elements are all there. But you need to underline your structure more clearly so the audience knows when they can go home. My advice to you is to take a step back and look at how the individual parts serve the whole. What's *A Strange Loop* about, who is it for, and why does it need be?

DIDN'T WANT NOTHIN'

Usher scribbles some ideas down.
And then there is Dad, carrying a forty-ounce bottle of beer.

THOUGHT 5:
HEY, SON, IT'S YOUR DAD

THOUGHT 6:
I DIDN'T WANT NOTHIN'

THOUGHT 2:
JUST THOUGHT I WOULD CALL

THOUGHTS 1 AND 2:
AND SAY

THOUGHT 4:
WASSUP

THOUGHT 5:
TO MY NUMBER ONE SON

THOUGHT 3:
IF YOU CALL ME BACK

THOUGHT 6:
I'LL GIVE YOU A NUMBER

THOUGHTS 1–3:
A NUMBER THAT ME

THOUGHTS 1–4:
>AND MOM

THOUGHTS 1–5:
>DUG UP

ALL THOUGHTS:
>OUT ON GOOGLES DOT COM
>I DON'T KNOW IF YOU KNOW WHO
>SCOTT RUDIN IS
>BUT I READ THAT EVEN HIS BALLS ARE PURE GOLD
>I DON'T MEAN TO GET
>ALL UP INTO YOUR BIZ
>BUT HOW ELSE YOU GONNA GET
>SUMMA O' YOUR WRITING SOLD
>
>I HEAR SCOTT'S A FAG
>Y'ALL GOT THAT IN COMMON

THOUGHTS 1, 3 AND 4:
>AND WHILE I DO NOT

THOUGHTS 1 AND 3:
>CONDONE

THOUGHT 6:
>GAY SEX

THOUGHT 5:
>YOU'VE GOT THAT FAT STUDENT LOAN

THOUGHT 2: All right, big guy, what am I going to say?
USHER: That my blood pressure is through the roof, my cholesterol is a disaster, and that I need to lose weight.

THOUGHT 2: Every year, it's the same notes but you don't seem to be getting it. You have such a cute face. Why on earth are you hiding it underneath all of this hideous blubber?

USHER: Can you just squeeze my nuts and have me cough again? I really enjoyed that.

THOUGHT 2: Have you had *any* dicks up your butt since I saw you last?

USHER: I average about one penetration once a year so my next one is bound to be any day now; that's just math.

THOUGHT 2: Pathetic. Even at the height of AIDS I was bouncing on every dick I could get my hands on, so what's your excuse?

USHER: Snagging a man is like finding affordable housing in this town—there's a long wait list and the landlords discriminate, okay? I'll just stick to porn in the meanwhile.

THOUGHT 2: Usher, as your doctor, I'm warning you that you absolutely must be getting sex more than once a year or you're putting yourself at risk.

USHER: At risk for what?

THOUGHT 2: At risk for not keeping up. You're a young gay living in the big city. This is your time! Too many beautiful men gave up their lives for you to not to be getting plowed and bred regularly. I'm writing you a prescription for Truvada as PrEP.

USHER: What the hell do I need Truvada for? The *last* thing I'm worried about is HIV!

THOUGHT 2: Oh, so you think you too *good* for HIV now! See, that's what you *not* gon' do. *Get* yo' fat ass outta here and *onto your phone.* By next year this time, I want to see that bootyhole o' yours tore up and worn *out* or I'ma fuck on you *myself*, and you won't like it when *I* get through with you, ya hear?

EXILE IN GAYVILLE

USHER *(Making a note)*: Usher enters the sexual marketplace.

(Usher's Thoughts enter.)

ALL THOUGHTS:
LOOKING? INTO? HUNG?

USHER: You can do this. You can do this.

ALL THOUGHTS:
LOOKING? INTO? HUNG?

USHER: It's just like double-dutch. Here we go.

INNER WHITE GIRL IT'S NO FUN
IN THIS AGE OF FUCK AND RUN
HEADLESS HORSEMEN CLOP AND FART
BE STILL MY SLEEPY, HOLLOW HEART
HERE I PRACTICE WHITE GIRL YOU
AND HOPE THAT ACT WILL GET ME THROUGH
WHILE STILL I'M STUCK INSIDE THIS SKIN
BUT ALSO OUTSIDE LOOKING IN
IT'S AN EXILE IN GAYVILLE HERE
FROM HELL'S KITCHEN TO SAYVILLE HERE
THEN A BUS THEN A FERRY THEN AN ORGY ON
   FIRE ISLAND
EXILE IN GAYVILLE HERE
TO PENN STATION FROM SAYVILLE HERE
FROM THE FRYING PAN INTO THE FIRE RAGING
   IN HELL'S KITCHEN
I HOPE THAT I GET BURNED

THOUGHTS 2–6:
> LOOKING? INTO? HUNG?

THOUGHT 6: Six foot two, a hundred seventy-nine pounds, muscular, single. Packing in the front and in the back. Able to take care of all your anal needs. Just say hi.

THOUGHTS 1, 3–6:
> LOOKING? INTO? HUNG?

THOUGHT 2: Undetectable poz bottom taking loads in the toilet on Lucky Burger on 52nd Street. Just steps away from Industry and Therapy. Come park it *right here*, gents. Don't be scared. Just say hi!

THOUGHTS 1–2, 4–6:
> LOOKING? INTO? HUNG?

THOUGHT 3: Laid back, nice guy here. No agenda, no drama. Just checking things out and maybe looking for a gym buddy lol. Top if it goes there. Just say hi!

USHER: . . . hi.

(No response; he waits and then speaks up:)

HI!

THOUGHT 1:
Too Black . . . THOUGHT 2:
Too Black . . . THOUGHT 3:
Too Black . . .

USHER: Hi. How are you tonight? Look at my ass.

THOUGHT 4:
Yr dick 2 small . . .   THOUGHT 5:
                         Yr dick 2 small . . .   THOUGHT 6:
                                                  Yr dick 2 small . . .

THOUGHT 1: Too Black.

THOUGHT 2: Too fat.

THOUGHT 3: Too feminine.

USHER: Well, maybe I could come over and we could just kiss then? I really like kissing.

THOUGHT 1: NO BLACKS!

THOUGHT 6: SORRY, GUY, EVERYBODY HAS A PREFERENCE!

USHER: Fine, *Scruff.*

THOUGHT 5: Fuck outta here, porch monkey!

USHER: Okay, *Grindr.*

THOUGHT 4: With those dingleberries? Boy, bye.

USHER: Fair enough, *Growlr.*

THOUGHT 3: When was the last time you got your bussy in formation with Beyoncé?

USHER: Not recently, *Adam4Adam*, because as a general rule, I don't fraternize with terrorists.

ALL THOUGHTS: Oh no she did NAWT just call Beyoncé a terrorist!

USHER: Oh, *yes*, she did!

ALL THOUGHTS:
BLOCK! BLOCK! BLOCK! BLOCK!
BLOCK! BLOCK! BLOCK! BLOCK!
BLOCK! BLOCK! BLOCK! BLOCK!

IS THAT SHADE YOU THROW A CRUTCH?
BITCH, YOU PROTEST TOO DAMN MUCH!

WHY SO SOUR? WHY SO STUCK?
DO OR DON'T YOU WANT TO FUCK?

(Cheerleading) Fuck! Fuck! Fuck! Fuck!

YES, YOU'RE UGLY, YES, YOU'RE FAT
BUT SOMEWHERE SOMEONE'S INTO THAT
SO DON'T BE SWINDLED BY SELF-DOUBT!
JUST KEEP ON SENDING DICK PICS OUT!

USHER AND ALL THOUGHTS:
IT'S AN EXILE IN GAYVILLE (YA FAGGOT)
FROM HELL'S KITCHEN TO SAYVILLE (YA FAGGOT)
THEN A BUS THEN A FERRY THEN AN ORGY ON
FIRE ISLAND
EXILE IN GAYVILLE (YA FAGGOT)
TO PENN STATION FROM SAYVILLE (YA FAGGOT)
FROM THE FRYING PAN
INTO THE FIRE RAGING
IN HELL'S KITCHEN
IN HELL'S KITCHEN
IN HELL'S KITCHEN
IN HELL'S KITCHEN

USHER:
I HOPE YOU FAGGOTS *BURN*!

(Gayville has an orgy to which Usher is not invited.)

USHER AND ALL THOUGHTS:
LOOKING? INTO? HUNG—

USHER:
—RY TO SHIT ON YOUR PALE LITTLE FACES

MICHAEL R. JACKSON

THOUGHT 5:

TOO BLACK TOO BLACK

USHER AND ALL THOUGHTS:

LOOKING? INTO? HUNG—

USHER:

—RY BUT PART OF ME WANTS TO TRADE PLACES

THOUGHT 5:

TOO FAT TOO FAT

USHER AND ALL THOUGHTS:

LOOKING? INTO? HUNG—

USHER:

—RY TO BURY THIS SEXUAL ANGUISH

ALL THOUGHTS:

YR DICK 2 SMALL! YR DICK 2 SMALL!

USHER AND ALL THOUGHTS:

LOOKING? INTO? HUNG—

USHER:

—RY TO CHOP OFF MY PENIS AND LANGUISH

ALL THOUGHTS:

TOO FAT! TOO BLACK! YR DICK 2 SMALL!
YR DICK 2 SMALL!

USHER:

MY DICK TOO SMALL! MY DICK TOO SMALL!
TOO FAT AND BLACK TO LIVE AT ALL!

SO WHY DON'T YOU JUST RAVAGE ME
WITH YOUR WHITE GAY DAN SAVAGERY?

(Usher steps onto a subway car, sits on one end of a three-seater, and notices Thought 3 wearing a matching tank top and neon-colored gym shoes, engrossed in something like Between the World and Me *or* The New Jim Crow. *Thought 5 enters, messenger bag akimbo. He sits next to Usher, who reviews a draft of* A Strange Loop. *Silence.)*

THOUGHT 5: What's a strange loop?

USHER: Huh?

THOUGHT 5: Oh, I'm sorry; I didn't mean to peek over your shoulder.

USHER: Oh. It's just the name of a musical I'm working on.

THOUGHT 5: You write musicals?

USHER: Yeah?

THOUGHT 5: Awesome. Did you see *Hamilton*?

USHER: I'm poor.

THOUGHT 5: Fair, fair. I only got to see it 'cause I used to date one of the King Georges.

USHER: Yay, King George.

THOUGHT 5: So *A Strange Loop*. What's the significance of the title?

USHER: Well, don't fall asleep but it's a cognitive-science term that was coined by this guy named Douglas Hofstadter. And it's basically about how your sense of self is just a set of meaningless symbols in your brain pushing up or down through one level of abstraction to another but always winding up right back where they started. It's the idea that your ability to conceive of yourself as an "I" is kind of an illusion. But the fact that you can recognize the illusion kind of proves that it exists. I don't totally get it. But it's also the name of this Liz Phair song I really love. Originally, I was gonna use a bunch of her songs in the show, but then she wouldn't give me permission. Her spirit lives on in the piece in other ways though.

THOUGHT 5: That is so funny. Liz is an alum of my high school. New Trier in Winnetka.

USHER: GET OUT! That's crazy! I mean, I went to *Cass Tech* in Detroit but New Trier is legendary too.

THOUGHT 5: Motor Town! Stand up, Detroit! *Exile in Guyville* is an incredible album. And your show sounds absolutely *tits*.

USHER: Thanks. Hopefully people will agree with you even though it's next to impossible to get folks excited about Black musicals that don't have us sha-la-la-ing in the background with bouffant wigs on or being blackfaced white characters but—

THOUGHT 5: I love your lisp. It's very sexy. So are you. I hope you don't mind my saying.

USHER: Wow. I so don't mind actually. Hi. I'm Usher.

THOUGHT 5: Ooh, a *famous name*. Nice to meet you, *Usher*. I'm *Joshlet*.

USHER: I can't with Joshlet. I'm jizzing all over myself. Really? *Joshlet?* That's adorbs.

THOUGHT 5: My parents are total faggots, what can I say?

USHER: Well, faggot or not, you're really hot if you don't mind my saying, Joshlet.

THOUGHT 5: Why thank you, sir. I don't mind you saying at all.

USHER: So this is totally not me but my place is at the last stop. Do you live in Queens?

THOUGHT 5: No, unfortunately, I live in your imagination.

USHER: Ah.

THOUGHT 5: I'm white obviously. Six foot one, with soft brown eyes, accidental six-pack abs, light brown scruff and an *exquisitely* groomed alt-right style haircut. I have an enormous pink cock, a full bush, and insanely low-hanging balls. In addition to being an obnoxious online thirst trap with millions of followers, I'm also a power top with a slight preference for piss play and came out to a supportive LGBTQIA-Plus-affirming church when I was eleven. Usher, what I like about you is how you're not afraid to let your sloppiness all hang out. And the fact that you would allow yourself even a moment of weakness to fantasize about a dick appointment with a Sean Cody–adjacent spawn of Satan like me when you should probably just kill yourself? Well, that's a testament to the awesome power of the white gaytriarchy.

(Pulls a Popeyes box out of his bag) Here. Have some Popeyes that I nutted on as a consolation prize.

(Tosses a Popeyes box on the floor like hog food; turns to Thought 3) Hey. Hey, you—Ink drop. What's your name, boy?

THOUGHT 3: *OhmyGod, it's totally Todrick and I swear I'm not as dark-skinned as I look.*

THOUGHT 5: That's okay, kid. When you're with me, you won't see color. And we're all just niggers when the lights go out anyway. So let's make a go of it, huh?

USHER: Indie rock guitar underscores them running off the train into the tangerine horizon of their Sundance Award–winning interracial gay movie love story tentatively titled *Love, Todrick.*

THOUGHT 1: Okay?

THOUGHT 6: Then what, bitch?

THOUGHT 2: Where's the sweat, Usher? You're not even trying!

USHER: I'm thinking!

THOUGHT 1: See that's really why nobody wants to fuck him.

THOUGHT 2: What is Usher's problem?

MICHAEL R. JACKSON

SECOND WAVE

USHER:

I DON'T HAVE AIDS
AND I DON'T CARE ABOUT MARRIAGE
AND I WILL NEVER BE PUSHING A LOUD-ASS BABY
AROUND IN A CARRIAGE
NO, I'LL JUST WALK AROUND WITH A SCOWL ON
    MY FACE LIKE I'M BETTY FRIEDAN
BECAUSE THE SECOND-WAVE FEMINIST IN ME
IS AT WAR WITH THE
DICK-SUCKING BLACK GAY MAN

WHO'S SOMETIMES LOOKING FOUR NOW
BUT ALSO FIFTEEN YEARS LATER
AND SO THE GRINDR CROWD TURNS ME INTO A
    CHRONIC
STAY-AT-HOME MASTURBATER
WHEN I WANT TO GO OUT ON A SATURDAY NIGHT
    I DON'T FEEL THAT I CAN
BECAUSE THE SECOND-WAVE FEMINIST IN ME
IS AT WAR WITH THE
DICK-SUCKING BLACK GAY MAN

SO I FALL OUTSIDE OF THE NORM
'CAUSE I BURN MY BRA TO KEEP WARM
WHILE MOST OF MY BRETHREN SWARM TO
BEYONCÉ AND RIHANNA
AND BAREBACK AND FELCHING AND SO ON

BUT THEY WON'T GET AIDS
'CAUSE NOW THEY'RE TAKING TRUVADA

AND I DON'T KNOW WHAT TO SAY SO I STAY IN
   MY CORNER
AND I JUST SAY NADA
AND WATCH THEM ALL DO WHAT THEY WANT
   WITHOUT FEAR AND WITHOUT HAVING A PLAN
MEANWHILE THE SECOND-WAVE FEMINIST IN ME
IS AT WAR WITH THE
DICK-SUCKING BLACK GAY MAN

SO NOBODY COMES ON MY CHEST
AND I COME OFF SOUNDING REPRESSED
BUT MAYBE THAT'S ALL FOR THE BEST
IF I WANT SOMETHING DEEPER
AND SOMEONE WHO THINKS I'M A KEEPER
AND WHO CAN UNDERSTAND MY LONG
   HESITATION
AND WHO WILL TAKE MY HAND AND HELP ME
   UNDO
THIS POLARIZATION
AND LETS ME CURL UP WITH CHARLENE,
   MARY JO, JULIA AND SUZANNE
UNTIL THE SECOND-WAVE FEMINIST IN ME
ENDS THE WAR WITH HIS
DICK-SUCKING BLACK GAY MAN

THOUGHT 3: Hey-hey! Usher! It's Agent Fairweather!
USHER: Hi, Agent Fairweather.

TYLER PERRY WRITES REAL LIFE

THOUGHT 3: I know it's been *months* since we last spoke and
I have no idea if this is of any interest to you or if you have
any material to send but we just got a call for submissions
for something very exciting. Especially for you.

USHER: Oh yeah? What is it?

THOUGHTS 4–6:
> TYLER

THOUGHTS 1–3:
> PERRY

THOUGHTS 4–6:
> TYLER

THOUGHTS 1–3:
> PERRY

THOUGHTS 4–6:
> TYLER PERRY

USHER: Oh, no!

THOUGHTS 4–6:
> TYLER

THOUGHTS 1–3:
> PERRY

THOUGHTS 4–6:
> TYLER

THOUGHTS 1–3:
> PERRY

THOUGHTS 4–6:
> TYLER PERRY

usher (*Mockingly sings à la* The Color Purple): Hellllll no!

thought 3: It seems he's gotten so busy with film and TV, that his team is looking to farm out the gospel plays to a ghostwriter. It'll be a scream. And didn't you once tell me that your mother would love nothing more than for you to write one? So how 'bout it, Ush? Just write a sassy matriarch, a lonely spinster who loves God; throw in a few *Color Purple* quotes, whaddaya say?

usher: What do I say? I say:

THANK YOU FOR THE OPPORTUNITY

thought 3: Of course, of course.

usher:

BUT TYLER WOULD BE NONE TOO FOND OF ME

thought 3: Don't sell yourself short.

usher:

THE CRAP HE PUTS ON STAGE, FILM AND TV
MAKES MY BILE WANNA RISE

thought 3: I know, "your integrity."

usher:

NOTHING THAT HE WRITES SEEMS REAL TO ME

thought 3: Yes, you think he sucks.

usher:

JUST SIMPLE-MINDLED, HACK BUFFOONERY

THOUGHT 3: But no theaters will touch you.

USHER:
AND IF I TRIED TO MATCH HIS COONERY
HE'D SEE THROUGH MY DISGUISE

THOUGHT 3: Just think about it.

USHER:
IT'S TRUE I'M STILL EMERGING
LOOKING TO MAKE MY START
BUT NOT SO HUNGRY THAT I'D
RIDE THE CHITLIN' CIRCUIT
I'M INTO ENTERTAINMENT
THAT'S UNDERCOVER ART
MY MISSION IS TO FIGURE OUT
JUST HOW TO WORK IT. TODAY
TODAY I PLAN TO CHANGE THIS SCENE FOR THE
    BETTER

(An unsettling sound.)

Hello? Agent Fairweather? Is somebody there?

(Voices from the darkness:)

THOUGHT 6: Race traitor . . .
THOUGHT 2: Race traitor . . .
THOUGHT 5: Race traitor . . .
USHER: Race traitor? Who's there?

(Voices from the darkness:)

THOUGHT 1: Ass licker . . .

THOUGHT 4: Ass licker . . .

THOUGHT 3: Ass licker . . .

USHER: Wh-wh-who are you?

(The Thoughts enter as Ancestors one by one.)

THOUGHT 2: I'm Harriet Motherfucking *Tubman*. And I got a problem wit' you.

THOUGHT 5: I'm Carter G. Motherfucking *Woodson* and I got a problem wit' you too.

THOUGHT 6: Jimmy Baldwin.

THOUGHT 3: Zora Neale Hurston.

THOUGHT 4: *Twelve Years a Slave* here.

(An entrance we won't soon forget.)

THOUGHT 1: Whitney.

USHER: W-w-w-what do you want with me?

THOUGHT 2: To get you together. Makin' me get MY Black ass up outta MY twenty-dollar grave to put YO' Black ass on blast talkin' bad 'bout Tyler Perry.

(The Ancestors get him together.)

ALL THOUGHTS:

WHO THE FUCK IS YOU, *NIGGUH*?
YOU LOOK IT BUT YOU AIN'T NO TRUE *NIGGUH*
YOU MAKE US ANCESTORS BLUE
ACTIN' BRAN'-NEW, *NIGGUH*, I CAIN'T WIT' YOU

TYLER IS A REAL *NIGGUH*
AND NOT A CRACKER-PLEASIN'-SEAL *NIGGUH*
HE WRITES HOW OUR PEOPLE FEEL

WITH HIM AT THE WHEEL;
NIGGUH, WHAT CAIN'T WE DO?

THOUGHTS 4–6:
'CAUSE TYLER PERRY WRITES REAL LIFE

THOUGHTS 1–3:
TYLER PERRY WRITES REAL LIFE

ALL THOUGHTS:
HE WRITES STORIES WE CAN SWALLOW LIKE
POPEYES CHICKEN AND BISCUITS

THOUGHT 2:
HE WRITES STORIES WE CAN FOLLOW LIKE WE
FOLLOWED THE DRINKING GOURD

ALL THOUGHTS:
HE WRITES STORIES 'BOUT FAT (UH-HUH) BLACK
WOMEN WIT' WEAVES (UH-HUH) FINDING
LOVE AND REDEMPTION
WIT' MUSCLE-BOUND BLACK MEN WHO OWN
THEY OWN BUSINESS AND TRULY LOVE THE
LORD! AND TRULY LOVE THE LORD!

SO IF YOU WON'T FOLLOW THROUGH, *NIGGUH*
I'LL SMDH AT YOU, *NIGGUH*

THOUGHT 3:
'CAUSE I'M JUST A SOMEBODY
TRY'NT TO TELL EVERYBODY
THAT YOU AIN'T NOBODY, NIGGUH, SO GET OFF
THE STAGE!

THOUGHTS 1–2, 4–6:	THOUGHT 3:
AND LET TYLER PERRY	AND LET TYLER PERRY
WRITE REAL LIFE!	WRITE REAL LIFE!
'CAUSE TYLER PERRY	'CAUSE TYLER PERRY
WRITES REAL . . .	WRITES REAL . . .
LIFE . . . OOH . . .	LIFE . . .
	(*À la* Good Times*:*)
	YEAHHHHHHH . . .

(All but Harriet Motherfucking Tubman exit.)

USHER: But his plays are worse for Black people than dia-fuckin'-betes!

THOUGHT 2: Diabeetus or not, he givin' niggas *jobs* and making niggas *money*, Usher. Money!

USHER: But "the master's tools will never dismantle the master's—"

THOUGHT 2: Find me Audre Lorde's dead bull-dyke ass on a map today. Now say sumpin' else.

USHER: Okay, okay, fine. I'll do it. But only for the money. And Mom. And Dad. And the ancestors.

THOUGHT 2: Good. 'Cause we the ones whose approval really matters.

　(Vigorously rubs her index finger back and forth against her knuckle) 'Cause o' *dis*. Ain't no "inner white girl" ever gonna let you get away from dis.

(Harriet Motherfucking Tubman exits. Usher takes a moment and then:)

WRITING A GOSPEL PLAY

USHER:

WRITING A GOSPEL PLAY!
WRITING A GOSPEL PLAY!
WRITING A GOSPEL PLAY!
'CAUSE THAT'S WHAT THE PEOPLE WANT!

Okay. Show title: *Show Me How to Pray*. A . . . *spiritual urban drama*.

(The Thoughts enter as the Quasi-Africana Church of God in Christ Choir.)

ALL THOUGHTS:

JUH-ESUS NUH-EVER FAILS
AS LONG AS YOU KEEP PRAYIN'
JUH-ESUS NUH-EVER FAILS
YOU THINK MY ASS IS PLAYIN'

(The Thoughts exit. Usher takes center stage to improv a gospel play.)

USHER *(As Aint Pattie)*: Shenithaaaa! Michelllllllle! I done made some "tata salaaaad"! C'mon now! I done put my foot in 'nis!

(As crazy Cousin Shenitha) UH OH AINT PETTIE!!!! I LUHHHHHH ME SOME "TATA SALAD" NAH AND I'M HONGRY AS HIZ-ZELLLLL!!!!!!!!!

(As Aint Pattie) Yo' fass behine ain't hongry for nuthin' but a crack rock and a stripper pole! Guhl, go wash yo' hand!

(As crazy Cousin Shenitha quoting The Real House-
wives of Atlanta*)* AINT PETTIE, ONLY GAWD CAN
JUDGE ME AND HE SEEMS QUITE IMPRESSED
SO DON'T COME FOR ME HAHAHAHA UNLESS
I *TWIRL* FOR YOU!!!!

(As Aint Pattie) 'Chel? What wrong, baby? You ain't
eatin' up ya "tata salad."

(As Michelle) Oh, Aint Pattie. How can I eat "tata salad"
when there's no *ring* on my finger?

(As crazy Cousin Shenitha) MICHELLE GRRRRRRL
YOU NEED TO FORGET ABOUT THAT RING
AND LEARN HOW TO DROP IT LIKE IT'S HOT!
HAHAHAHA!!!!!!

(As Aint Pattie admonishing crazy Cousin Shenitha) Fix
it, Jesus.

(As Michelle in a depressed stupor) I did everything I was
supposed to. I stayed in school? I kept my legs close? I was
faithful and paid my tithes and offering because Mark 12
and 17 says, "Render to Caesar the things that are Caesar's and to God the things that are God's."

(As crazy Cousin Shenitha) GAWD SAY, "BITCH BETTA
HAVE MAH MONEY RIGHT CHEA!" HAHAHA!

(As Aint Pattie) Guhl if you don't saddown I'ma pop
you in the face wit' one o' my *world-famous* Pattie pies!

(As crazy Cousin Shenitha) DID SOMEBODY SAY
PETTIE PIE? I'M HONGRY AS HIZ-ZELLLLL
HAHAHAHAHA!!!!!!!!!

(As Michelle) I wore flesh-colored stockings? I got a
perm? Then a wig that I put on *top* of the perm as a pro-
tective style? I became a high-powered vice president of a
bank? But I'm still so, so lonely!!!!!!

(As Aint Pattie comforting her) Oh, baby! Rest yo' head
on Aint Pattie bosom.

(As Michelle) When is it *my* turn to walk into a room and say, "I's married nah, Miss Celie!"?

(As Aint Pattie very serious) Well, have you prayed?

(As Michelle earnestly pouring her heart out to Aint Pattie) I get down on my Black knees every night!

(As crazy Cousin Shenitha being triflin' for no reason) I KNOW WHAT I DO DOWN ON *MAH* BLACK KNEES GURL!!! MMKAY???

(As Aint Pattie teaching/preaching an important lesson) Well, if you getting down on your knees and the Lord idn't blessin' ya the way ya think he ought to then . . .

MAYBE YOU DON'T KNOW HOW TO PRAY

ALL THOUGHTS:

MAYBE YOU DON'T KNOW (HOW TO PRAY)

USHER:

MAYBE YOU DON'T KNOW HOW TO PRAY

ALL THOUGHTS:

MAYBE YOU DON'T KNOW HOW TO PRAY

USHER:

IN TIMES LIKE DEEZ YA GOTTA GET DOWN ON
    YO' KNEES
AND ASK HIM FOR THE WORDS YOU SHOULD SAY

ALL THOUGHTS:

ASK HIM FOR THE WORD, YEAH!

USHER *(As Aint Pattie)*:
And I know you feel like your Cousin Shenitha doin' better 'n' you 'cause she be out there prostitutin' herself to all these mens who be touching her on the vagina. And I know you feel like your Cousin Shereé doin' better 'n' you 'cause she got the money to build herself a chateau in Atlanta but remember Proverbs 31 and 10 says: "*Who can find a virtuous woman? For her price is far above rubies,*" so keep your knees bent in prayer and the Lord thy God will send you a light-skinded man with no education who will put you in the split-level mansion of your dreams, Chel!!!!!!

ALL THOUGHTS *(On loop)*:
PRAY! PRAY, PRAY! PRAY! PRAY-PRAY! PRAY!

THOUGHTS 5 AND 6:
YOU GOT TO . . .

ALL THOUGHTS:
PRAY!
PRAY! PRAY, PRAY! PRAY! PRAY-PRAY! PRAY!

THOUGHTS 5 AND 6:
YOU GOT TO . . .
PRAY! PRAY, PRAY! PRAY! PRAY-PRAY! PRAY!

USHER *(As Michelle)*:
   AINT PATTIE, ALL I REALLY WANT IS A RING

ALL THOUGHTS:
   RING!

USHER *(As crazy Cousin Shenitha)*:
   MAYBE THE DEVIL GOT YO' ASS IN A SLING;
   HAHAHAHAHA!

ALL THOUGHTS:
   SLING, SLING, SLING . . .

USHER (*As Aint Pattie*):
> ON DAYS LIKE DEEZ IT'S LIKE YOU TRAPPED ON A
> TRAPEZE AND YOU

THOUGHTS 3–6:
> DAYS LIKE OOH . . .

THOUGHTS 1 AND 2:
> YEAH, YEAH, YEAH, YEAH, YEAH!

USHER: Don't know what these dumb-ass paper doll "characters" should sing!!!!!!!

ALL THOUGHTS:
> JUH-ESUS NUH-EVER FAILS . . .

USHER (*Waves away the Thoughts*): Enough! Shut up! I gotta get my Black ass to work!

(Usher rings the intermission chimes. Thought 1 waves at Usher, trying to get his attention.)

THOUGHT 1: Usher! Excuse me, usher! How many minutes 'til the end of intermission?
USHER: About two more minutes I'd say?
THOUGHT 1: How many times have you seen the show?
USHER: More times than I care to count.
THOUGHT 1: Is this your full-time job?
USHER: Yes, ma'am.
THOUGHT 1: It probably doesn't pay very much I would imagine, but you probably do it because you love the theater so much, right?
USHER: Uh-huh.

THOUGHT 1: Oh, I see. Well, what is *your* big New York City dream?

USHER: To be a musical theater writer.

THOUGHT 1: Really! A musical *theater* writer! How wonderful! My goodness! Musicals are just the most magical things, wouldn't you say?

USHER: Magical or infuriating, depending on which side of it you're on I suppose.

THOUGHT 1: Having a bit of writer's block?

USHER: Something like that.

THOUGHT 1: Would it help to talk through it?

USHER: Huh. Well . . . it's about a Black gay man writing a musical about a Black gay man who's writing a musical about a Black gay man who's writing a musical about a Black gay man, etc. And now I've gotten to the part of the story where he wants to share his artistic self with his parents which is weirdly harder than sharing his sexual self which he also skirts around because of how traumatic coming out was in the first place when he was seventeen and I keep feeling like he needs to confront them about *all* of it as one experience but I'm scared to write that because then I might have to do it in real life or maybe I'm scared to do that in real life because then I might have to write it? Does that make any sense or am I just being totally stupid?

THOUGHT 1: My, my. You're certainly a *radical* young man aren't you?

USHER: That's what my mom always says.

THOUGHT 1: Well, since you asked, I don't think you're being totally stupid but I do think you might be overcomplicating.

USHER: How so?

A SYMPATHETIC EAR

THOUGHT 1:

I LIKE THIS AND I LIKE *WICKED* . . .
I COME UP EVERY YEAR TO SEE MY SHOWS
I'M FROM MIAMI BEACH
YOU KNOW, FROM FLORIDA
LIKE DOROTHY, BLANCHE, S'PHIA, *AND* ROSE

ALL MY LIFE I LIVED FOR OTHERS
MADE SPACE FOR EVERY DREAM EXCEPT MY OWN
BUT THEN ONE DAY I LOOKED INTO THE MIRROR
AND SAW THAT I WAS OLD AND ALL ALONE

SO MY ADVICE: DON'T PLAY NICE
DON'T LOOK BACK AND DON'T THINK TWICE
DON'T LET DOUBT GET IN THE WAY OF WHAT
    YOU WANT;
JUST ROLL THE DICE
STAY THE COURSE . . . SEIZE THE DAY
RIDE THE HORSE INTO THE FRAY
LIVE YOUR LIFE AND TELL YOUR STORY
    IN EXACTLY THE SAME WAY:
TRUTHFULLY AND WITHOUT FEAR!
DESPITE THOSE WHO WISH YOU WOULD
    DISAPPEAR
FIND JOY INSIDE YOUR LIFE WHILE YOU'RE STILL
    HERE
THAT'S YOUR CHALLENGE FROM A SYMPATHETIC
    EAR . . .

If you're not scared to write the truth then it's probably not worth writing. And if you're not scared of living the truth then it's probably not worth living. Do you understand?

USHER: I think so?

(A beat. Thought 1 exits. Usher makes a note.)

Usher calls home.

THOUGHT 6: My son! Well, look at that! You don't hardly never call home!

USHER: I'm just calling for some love.

THOUGHT 6: Calling for some love, huh? Well, your mom's not here.

USHER: I don't have to talk to Mom; I can talk to you.

THOUGHT 6: Oh, okay. Well, what's good, my son? Tell me about your personal life. You ain't went and got AIDS, have you?

USHER: No, but play your cards right and maybe that's what I'll bring you home next Christmas.

THOUGHT 6: Okay, Mr. Comedian. But that A-word is *real*. Remember your cousin Darnell?

USHER: Dad, don't talk about Darnell like that.

THOUGHT 6: I'm just saying. You keep living that lifestyle and God will punish you with that—

THOUGHT 2: MUFASAAAAA!!!

THOUGHT 6: Sarabi, goddamn! What the hell is wrong wit' you?

THOUGHT 2: What's wrong is yo' grandbaby's airheaded mama went in the church parking lot and spray-painted "see you next Tuesday" on my *vee*-hickle!!!!!

THOUGHT 6: "See you next Tuesday"?!?

THOUGHT 2: "See you next Tuesday"! "Cunt!"

THOUGHT 6: Sarabi, stop shouting and say hi to your baby boy while I go look at this damn car!

(Thought 6 exits.)

THOUGHT 2: Cunt, cunt, cunt! Lord, I'm so glad Nala cain't read yet! But let me hush! How's my chile? Any producers give you the hookup on your musical the-a-ter writings yet?

USHER: Not yet, Mom.

THOUGHT 2: That's why you need to turn our babymamadrama into a reality show! 'Cause on top o' everything else, Rafficki been going around tellin' diff'rent people at church like that airheaded Marion that the only reason she even wound up pregnant wit' Nala in the first place is 'cause Scar raped her!

THOUGHT 3: Ma! I ain't rape nobody! And why you always gotta put somebody business out in the street!

THOUGHT 2: Scar, you live in our basement, don't pay not one penny o' rent, eat up all our food and ain't paid chile support in six months so you ain't *got* no business!

THOUGHT 3: At least I ain't up in New York lettin' no niggas give me AIDS! What y'all gon' do when yo' baby boy wind up wit' AIDS like Darnell?!?

THOUGHT 6: Well, it's right there on the side! "Cunt!" But I can get that painted over! Hey, Scar! Go 'n' look at what yo' babymama did to your mom's vehicle!

THOUGHT 3 *(As he exits)*: Maaaaan . . .

THOUGHT 2: Hey, Mufasa! Usher still cain't get the hookup wit' his musical the-a-ter writings!

THOUGHT 6: Hey Son, maybe you should write more like how Tyler Perry writes! Now *that* nigga knows how to write for the Blacks and make the money!

THOUGHT 2: Oh no! Usher *too good* for Black folks and money! And he don't seem to get that God blessed Tyler and sent him to Earth to be our voice along with Barack!

(Usher opens his laptop and begins to write the scene.)

THOUGHT 3: Rafficki!

THOUGHT 1: Nigga, *prove* I spray-painted yo' bitch-ass mama car!

THOUGHT 2: No cursing, no cursing!

THOUGHT 3: That's why you ain't *never* gettin' this dick again!

THOUGHT 2: This is a house of the Lord(t)!

THOUGHT 1: Maybe if you wadn't layin' up in the bed wit' all kinda women and put a *ring* on my finger, you—

THOUGHT 2:	THOUGHT 3:
Would you bring me some Popeyes, Mufasa?	Bitch, I lay up in the bed wit' who I want!
THOUGHT 6:	THOUGHT 1:
It's in the kitchen on the stove! You got legs!	Nigga, we have a chiiiiile together and this is how you want her to see our family?
THOUGHT 2:	THOUGHT 3:
Mufasa, would you *be nice* and go in the kitchen and put some Popeyes on a plate with a biscuit for your wife please?!?	We ain't never gon' be a *family*, you toxic-ass chickenhead trick!

THOUGHT 2: Usher! You writin' all this down? This our babymamadrama reality show!

THOUGHT 6: I'm gone upstairs! Y'all niggas give me a headache!

THOUGHT 2: Them beers giving you the headache! And what you gone upstairs for? I ain't got through tellin' Usher how Scar *"raped"* Rafficki!

THOUGHT 6: Usher, do you think Scar raped Rafficki?!?!?

THOUGHT 2: Did I say that Scar raped Rafficki?!?!?

THOUGHT 6: Yeah, you said Scar raped Rafficki!!!!

THOUGHT 2: Naw, I ain't!

THOUGHT 6: Yes, you did!

THOUGHT 2: Naw, I *ain't*!!!!

THOUGHT 6: *Sarabi, yes you did!!!!*

THOUGHT 2: I ain't say that Scar raped Rafficki; I said that Rafficki *said* that Scar raped—

USHER: Oh, what difference does it make? What the fuck diff—

THOUGHT 2: Who the "f" is you, Negro? Sittin' up there cussin' and carryin' on, actin' like you ain't got no good home trainin' wit' yo' musical the-A-ter writings and Doodoo Bank Student Loans callin' MY house in the middle of da night lookin' for money for YO' Black butt and you cain't even get Toya to get rid o' her huzzzband and have a baby for you 'cause you too busy sittin' up there in the homosexsh'alities and prob'ly hidin' that you got AIDS from everybody like Darnell was.

(A screeching atomic explosion of a tantrum; separate claps on "still," "ain't," "got," "my," "gospel":)

AND I *STILL.* AIN'T. GOT MY GOSPEL PLAYYYY-YYYYYYYY!!!!!!!!!!!!!!!!

(A pause; composes herself; an eerily low voice; the final TKO:)

But that's not what's *important* in this household. What's *important* is *(All her venom turns to Mufasa)* for *YO' DAAAAD* to come be-boppin' in here tellin' me that I said Scar raped Rafficki when I KNOW what I said was, was that *Rafficki(!!!)* said that Scar raped Rafficki.

(Silence.)

THOUGHT 1: Dayum. Listening to this bitch run her mouf done got my pussy to poppin' sumpin' *crazy*! You ready to go down in dat basement and get you some?

THOUGHT 3: Yeah, bitch, c'mon.

(Thoughts 1 and 3 exit.)

THOUGHT 6: Here's your *got-damn* Popeyes.

THOUGHT 2: It's not warm. And would you bring me some hot sauce outta the kitchen please? Since you ain't feel like gettin' me *spicy* Popeyes like I ast you?

THOUGHT 6: Hey, Sarabi?

THOUGHT 2: What.

THOUGHT 6: See you next Tuesday.

THOUGHT 2: Usher, let me call you back.

　　(No response; looking around) Hello? Hello? Usher? Usher! Usherrrrrr!!!!!

(Usher takes out his chimes.)

THOUGHT 4: Hi, Usher, it's Mom. Guess who died? You don't have to call me back unless you wanna know who it is. Bye!

(Usher chimes and then:)

THOUGHT 2: Usher! It's your Daily Self-Loathing here! Don't forget how fat and ugly you are! Of course Darnell was pretty and he *still* died of AIDS so good luck, sis.

(Usher chimes and then:)

THOUGHT 3: Usher, Agent Fairweather. Any updates on a draft of *Show Me How to Pray?*

(Usher chimes and then:)

THOUGHT 1: Usher, as supervisor of your sexual ambivalence I'm fighting as valiantly as I can but I don't know how much longer we can protect your precious butthole from the colonizers!

(Usher chimes. And then:)

THOUGHT 5: Hey, Son, it's your dad. 'Member when you first told us you was "attracted to men"? And I asked you, I said, "You say you attracted to men. Well, I'm a man. Are you attracted to me?" I ain't gon' stop askin' 'til I get an answer, Son.

INWOOD DADDY

Thought 6 welcomes Usher into his apartment.

THOUGHT 6: Usher?
USHER: I'm so sorry I'm so late. The MTA sucks and Inwood is never as easy to navigate as I think it's gonna be.
THOUGHT 6: That's okay. Because who knows the next time I'll be able to get away from my wife for one of my little New York City rendezvous like this, so let's get this party started. You smoke, bro?
USHER: No.
THOUGHT 6: Well, I'm gonna smoke myself up a little.

(Thought 6 opens a drawer and pulls out meth and a pipe. He lights up. The other Thoughts enter eavesdropping on the scene.)

USHER: Um, is that crack?

THOUGHT 6: No, dummy, it's meth, and if you don't want to be here, I've got blacker asses than yours lined up for days in my Gmail.

USHER *(Steps out of the moment)*:

I ALWAYS SAY I PLAN TO CHANGE MY LIFE TODAY
BUT THE ONLY THING I EVER SEEM TO DO
IS WRITE A SONG
IS WRITE A SONG
IS WRITE A SONG
BUT TONIGHT I GOT ATTRACTED TO

THOUGHTS 1–3:

INWOOD DADDY SUCKING COCK ALL SATURDAY
     MORNING

THOUGHTS 1–5:

INWOOD DADDY SUCKING COCK ALL SATURDAY
     MORNING

USHER:

HE POSTED

THOUGHT 6:

"IT'S MY GUARANTEE YOU'LL HAVE THE TIME OF
     YOUR LIFE, BRO;
WANNA GIVE OUT SOME DICK I DON'T EVEN GIVE
     TO MY WIFE SO

ALL BLACKS AND LATINOS
TO THE FRONT OF THE LINE
IF YOU GIMME THAT FAT BUBBLE BUTT,
I'LL TREAT IT JUST LIKE A SHRINE . . ."

USHER: No, it's fine. Sorry for being such a "See You Next Tuesday." Smoke all you want.

THOUGHT 6: That is just the sexiest fucking lisp. It makes you sound like a baby. I fucking *love* babies. How old are you?

USHER: Twenty-five. I turn twenty-six tomorrow actually.

THOUGHT 6: Huh. I would have guessed fourteen or fifteen.

USHER: Oh, yeah. I get that a lot. None of that hard living I guess.

THOUGHT 6: Well let's get you into that birthday suit so we can celebrate then, big guy. You've taken care of business back there, right? I know most of you boys don't wash but when I get to pound town I like a clean workspace.

USHER: I did my best, okay? Um, do you have something to wrap that up with?

THOUGHT 6: Let me get you some poppers.

USHER: I'm sorry. I'm just a little shy about drugs.

THOUGHT 6 (*Mocks Usher's lisp*): Poppers isn't "*drugs*"! C'mon! It'll open up that sweet potato pie of yours.

USHER: No, I'm sorry. And please. Wrap it up. I'm sorry. I'm not on PrEP.

THOUGHT 6: *Jesus Christ*. Aight. But you know how thick I am so don't come cryin' to me when you go into prolapse after I blow that hole out.

USHER: You gonna blow my hole out, daddy?

THOUGHT 6: Oh, most definitely, my dude.

(*Usher steps outside of himself as Thought 6 undresses.*)

USHER:

I ALWAYS SAY I PLAN TO CHANGE MY LIFE TODAY
AND THAT'S EXACTLY WHAT I'M ABOUT TO DO
BUT IS IT WRONG?
AND AM I WRONG?
IS IT WRONG?
AM I WRONG TO BE ATTRACTED TO

USHER:	THOUGHTS 1–3:
THE WHITE MALE INDIFFERENCE CROSSED WITH FETISHIZATION? WHICH IS EASY TO DO WHEN YOU'RE FEELING SUCH DESPERATION . . .	THE WHITE MALE INDIFFERENCE CROSSED WITH FETISHIZATION? WHICH IS EASY TO DO WHEN YOU'RE FEELING SUCH DESPERATION . . .

(Usher slowly undresses.)

THOUGHTS 1–5:

'CAUSE YOU'RE JUST A DUMB MONKEY AND THE
PAIN OF THAT HAUNTS YOU

THOUGHTS 1–3:

SO JUST DO WHAT HE SAYS

THOUGHTS 4–5:

BECAUSE AT LEAST SOMEONE WANTS YOU . . .

(The Thoughts begin a sexy minstrel dance around the sex act.)

THOUGHT 6:	USHER:	THOUGHTS 1–5:
You like my white	Mmmmm . . .	WHITE. WHITE.
cock in your ass	mmmm . . .	WHITE. WHITE.
don't you, nigger?	uhhhhhh . . .	WHITE. WHITE.
The niggers	ooh . . . ahhh . . .	WHITES ONLY.
always love it	uh, uh, uh . . .	WHITE. WHITE.
when I give 'em		WHITE. WHITE.
a little police		WHITE. WHITE.
brutality up the		WHITES ONLY.
old Hershey		
Hideaway . . .		
Open up for me,	Yes, fuck my	JIM CROW.
blacky. Oooopen	bussy. Fuck my	JIM CROW.
up for me. Thass	bussy, daddy. Fuck	BE HIS
right, yeah, yeah.	my bussy, fuck my	WHITE. WHITE.
Ahhhh . . .	bussy, give me that	WHITE. WHITE.
(Pounds him in	good gutter sex,	WHITE. WHITE.
silent ecstasy for a	daddy; give me	WHITES ONLY.
while, then)	that gutter sex.	BE HIS
Aw, Kunta Kinte,	Uh, uh, uh, uh,	WHITE. WHITE.
those aren't tears in	uh . . .	WHITE. WHITE.
your eyes, are they?	No.	WHITE. WHITE.
		WHITES ONLY.
Is Massa making	No.	JIM CROW.
you KWYYY?	*(Howling with the*	JIM CROW.
	Gayville minstrels)	(BE HIS
Good 'cause I like	IT'S THE ONLY	WHITE. WHITE.
it *rough*. And now	THING I EVER	WHITE.
Massa's gonna	SEEM TO DO . . .	NIGGER . . .)
fuck you 'til you		BE HIS NIGGER
learn to be a good	IT'S THE ONLY	BE HIS NIGGER
little boyyyyy . . .	THING I EVER	BE HIS NIGGER
(Pounding him)	SEEM TO DO . . .	GIVE HIM

THOUGHT 6		THOUGHTS 1–5
(Continued):	USHER	*(Continued)*:
Take it, monkey.	*(Continued)*:	THAT FAT,
Take my dick, take	IT'S THE ONLY	BLACK ASS . . .
my dick, take my	THING I EVER	BE HIS
dick, take my . . .	SEEM TO DO . . .	NIGGER . . .
(Moaning/groaning)	BE HIS	GIVE HIM
fuuuuck . . .	NIGGER	THAT FAT,
yeahhh . . .	NIGGER . . .	BLACK ASS . . .
(Continues pounding	*(Usher has a weak*	NIGGER . . .
the shit out of him	*orgasm)*	
until he comes all		
over Usher's back)		

(Long silence.)

THOUGHT 6: That was so nice. *(Exhales, satisfied)* I mean you're still learning . . . but that was really lovely. I love teaching young boys how to use their bodies. *(Yawns)* You really should use poppers though if you're not gonna tweak, bro. It makes it *so* much better.

USHER: Well, I hope you don't mind but I have *so* much work to do.

THOUGHT 6: It's Sunday.

USHER: A LOT of work to do.

THOUGHT 6: What do you do for work?

USHER: It's too boring to talk about.

THOUGHT 6: C'mon. Stay. I can make breakfast. You like grits? I make great grits. And I think I have some leftover Popeyes from the last boy that was here.

(Finds it; hands Usher a box of Popeyes) Yyyyep. Here it is. Want?

USHER: Look. I hate to make this a fuck-and-run but thanks for a fun night. It was amaze.

THOUGHT 6: Sure but text me sometime. For you, I'd figure out how to make my little New York City getaways a semi-regular thing.

USHER: You're sweet.

THOUGHT 6: *Seriously*. You have a really hot ass.

BOUNDARIES

USHER:
WHY DID I DO THAT?
WHAT DID THAT DO FOR ME?
WHAT A PERFORMANCE
WHERE ARE MY BOUNDARIES?

I THREW MY HANDS UP
HE BLEW MY HOUSE DOWN
ALL I EVER WANTED WAS TO JUMP OFF OF A
    PRECIPICE
LAUNCH MY GOLDEN PARACHUTE
A WIN FOR THE RECORD BOOK
THOUGHT I HAD WHAT IT TOOK
NOT AS SMART AS I LOOK
'CAUSE NOW I'M PRACTICALLY IN TRACTION

WHY DID I DO THAT?
DOWN ON MY HANDS AND KNEES?
WHY PLAY SUBMISSIVE?
WHAT ARE MY BOUNDARIES?

THOUGHT IT WOULD LEARN ME
IF I LET IT BURN ME
ALL I EVER WANTED WAS TO SHOW THAT I WAS
    TOUGH ENOUGH

BIG ENOUGH AND STRONG ENOUGH TO
SLOW DOWN A SPEEDING TRAIN
OUTRUN THE BULLS IN SPAIN
I SWERVED OUTSIDE MY LANE
MY BRAKES WENT OUT AND NOW I'M ROADKILL

STILL I BEAT MYSELF UP
STILL I KNOCK MYSELF DOWN
AND STILL I FLIP MYSELF OFF IN THE MIRROR
WHICH MAKES ME FEEL REALLY BAD
WHICH MAKES ME FEEL REALLY GOOD
WHICH MAKES ME FEEL LIKE THE STUPIDEST
    ASSHOLE
RUBBER WANTS TO HIT THE OPEN ROAD
BUT I KEEP DWELLING ON THE PAST
I PRAY THAT SOME DAY I WILL CHANGE
STRANGER THINGS HAVE HAPPENED
EACH TIME I TRY TO CHART MY COURSE
WILD HORSES THROW ME OFF BY FORCE

THE SAME OLD STORY
LURCHING AFTER GLORY
AND I FALL SHORT

WHY DO I DO THIS?
BOW DOWN AND PEOPLE-PLEASE
I CAN'T KNOW FREEDOM
WITHOUT CLEAR BOUNDARIES
'TIL I DRAW BOUNDARIES
I HAVE NO BOUNDARIES

PERIODICALLY

USHER: Usher's walk of shame from Inwood takes him deeper into a strange loop, which is precisely the moment he gets his annual birthday voicemail from Mom.

(Thought 4 enters dressed like a gospel play matriarch.)

THOUGHT 4:
I JUST LIKE TO REMIND YOU PERIODICALLY
THAT I LOVE YOU, SON
IF YOU EVER SHOULD FIND YOU
NEED ENCOURAGEMENT
THEN YOU CALL ME, SON
I AM YOUR MAMA
AND I'VE ALWAYS LOVED YOU
EVEN WHEN YOU BE DOING ME WRONG
I WENT THROUGH LABOR
HOURS OF LABOR
TO BRING YOU ALONG
AND YOU MEAN ALL THE WORLD TO ME
YOU MEAN ALL THE WORLD TO ME
YOU'RE THE REASON I'M SINGING THIS SONG
THIS IS THE DAY! THIS IS THE DAY!
THIS IS THE DAY THAT THE LORD HAS MADE!
(A cappella:)
THAT THE LORD HAS MADE!
HE HAS A MILESTONE IN MY BABY'S LIFE—YOU
    TURNED TWENTY-SIX OOON THE TWENTY-SIX!
AAAAAND THIS WILL NEVER HAPPEN AGAIIIIN!
SOOOOO ENJOY YOUR DAYYYY!

You were born at 8:31 this morning, my love. Mom loves you. You turned twenty-six on the twenty-six. Can't tell you *nuthin'*! May you have a good day—I know it's early! I hope I'm the first one to call ya! But even if I'm not, with the exception of our dear Heavenly Father, I'm the one that loves you the most. Well, me AND your dad. Okay, my love? Aw, I know, I'm gettin' all sen-i-men-al and mush but we be *thinkin'* about you and we be *prayin'* about you 'cause I get *worried*(!) with my baby up there in New York with folks livin' any which o' way. Like them folks on *Entertainment Tonight*. Do you watch *Entertainment Tonight*? I sure hope you don't wit' different people sittin' up there talkin' 'bout Michael Jackson fiddlin' with little boys and R. Kelly fiddlin' with little girls and Botox and *abortion*? But I know I don't have to worry about *my* baby bein' Botoxed and aborted 'cause *my* baby was raised in the fear and admonition of the Lord! And the Proverbs which says: "Raise up a child in the way he should go and he will not depart from it."

I JUST LIKE TO REMIND YOU
PERIODICALLY, READ YOUR BIBLE, SON
DON'T PUT JESUS BEHIND YOU
PERIODICALLY, READ YOUR BIBLE, SON
ONE—HONOR THY FATHER
AND THY MOTHER
THAT THY DAYS ON THE EARF WILL BE LONG
TWO—BE YE ENCOURAGED
YE MAY FEEL HELPLESS
BUT JESUS IS STRONG!!!
AND THREE!—AND MOST IMPORTANTLY
AND MOST IMPORTANTLY
IT'S THE REASON I'M SINGING THIS SONG

Listen at me now:

MAN IS FOR WO-MAN

USHER: His mom starts on her sermonizing.

THOUGHT 4:
AND WO-MAN FOR MAN!

USHER: Aw, shucky ducky nah!

THOUGHT 4:
THE REST IS CONFUSION!

USHER: Tell it lak it is, tell it lak it is!

THOUGHT 4:
AND NOT IN GOD'S PLAN!

USHER: That's right! That's right! That's right! Ooooooh,
Lordy! YOU BETTA SANG, MOTHA!

THOUGHT 4:
ALL O' THESE HOLLYWOOD HOMOSEXUALS!
WAVING GAY FLAGS ALL DAY AND NIGHT!
STICKING THEY THANGS UP EACH OTHER'S
BUTTHOLES!
I'M TELLING YOU, SON, THAT IT JUST AIN'T
RIGHT!
IT AIN'T RIGHT! IT AIN'T RIGHT! IT AIN'T RIGHT
WIT' GAWD!
IT AIN'T RIGHT! IT AIN'T RIGHT! IT AIN'T RIGHT
WIT' ME!

AND I JUST LIKE TO CALL UP MY BABY BOY
AND REMIND HIM OF THAT PERIODICALLY . . .

USHER AND THOUGHT 4:
'CAUSE I LOVE YOU
AND I DON'T WANT YOUR SOUL TO BE WASTED
IT HURTS ME SO BAD SOMETIMES I CAN TASTE IT
HELL IS REAL . . .
SINNERS BURNING . . .
SINNERS CHURNING IN RIVERS OF FIRE . . .
'CAUSE O' FILTHY, UNHOLY DESIRE . . .
HELL IS REAL!
THOUGH WE LOVE YOU . . .
DON'T REPENT 'CAUSE YOU KNOW IT WOULD
    PLEASE US . . .

SON, YOU SHOULD DO IT SO YOU CAN SEE JESUS . . .
HE IS REAL!
AND HE LOVES YOU . . .
AND HE DON'T WANT YOUR SOUL TO BE WASTED . . .
'CAUSE ALL DA PAIN OF THE WORLD, HE DONE
    FACED IT . . .
HE IS REAL!
AND I LOVE HIM . . .
SO DESPITE ALL MY PAIN AND MY STRIFE I'LL
    JUST KEEP ON PRAYING YOUR REPROBATE
    LIFESTYLE . . .
ISN'T REAL . . .

(Thought 4 exits.)

THOUGHT 2: Happy birthday, Usherrrrr!
USHER: Go away, Daily Self-Loathiiiiiing.

THOUGHT 2 (*À la Wendy Williams*): HOW U DOIN'?

USHER: What do you care?

THOUGHT 2: Oh, I don't. But I had some time to kill so I just thought I'd drop by to remind you how truly worthless you—

USHER: Fuck you.

THOUGHT 2: Naw, nigguh, fuck *you*. I'm just stating a fact. Some people never change. Certainly not a little *fat-ass* darkie like you.

USHER: Oh yeah? Well, we'll see about that.

THOUGHT 2: Well, look at God! So what's next, you little masochist?

(Thought 5 enters dressed like a gospel play patriarch.)

DIDN'T WANT NOTHIN' (REPRISE)

THOUGHT 5:

HEY, SON, IT'S YOUR DAD
I DIDN'T WANT NOTHIN'
JUST THOUGHT I WOULD CALL
AND SAY WASSUP
TO MY SECOND-BORN SON

SOME PEOPLE AT CHURCH
SAW SOME O' YOUR MUSIC
IT'S OUT THERE ONLINE
OUT FRONT JUST LIKE
SOMEBODY SPRAY-PAINTED "CUNT" . . .

THOUGHT 4: Airhead Marion comin' up to me at church wit' a smirk on her dat-blasted face talkin' 'bout: "We heard Usher music, Sister Sarabi. He always been real talented.

Too bad he all off into the homosexsh'alities. I hope God don't punish him wit' AIDS like he did Darnell."

THOUGHT 5: Awww, who care about all'at who-shot-John bullshit?

THOUGHT 4: *I* CARE!!!!!

THOUGHT 5: WELL, YOU *SHOULDN'T*! Marion ain't nothin' but a damn *slut* so I don't give a damn *what* she got to say! And if Usher wonts to write about kissin' on men and mess around and get hisself AIDS doin' what the white man wonts him to do wit' his asshole and go against God's word then who the fuck are we? So what *else* is goin' on in New York, Son? Tell me about your personal life. How many dicks you been suckin'? You been slurpin' any come down y'throat? What about that guy Toya supposedly married to? You been fuckin' on that nigguh? He been fuckin' on you?

USHER: No. Toya's husband hasn't been *fucking on* me and I haven't been *fucking on* him. They're happily married and that's not about to change any time soon. And while there is not *currently* any semen in my stomach, yes, I'm still "all off into the homosexsh'alities." But all that really means is that on the rare occasions I do end up taking my clothes off in front of someone, it's usually for some raggedy-ass white man who gets to nut all over me even though all *I* really want is to be with a Black man who rides for me as much as I ride for him. Especially when the anti-Black world we live in gets so strung out on this color-blind "love is love" bullshit, forgetting that "love is love" will never be true until *Black* love matters and *Black* lust matters and *Black* queers can *finally* stop using white men to flatter or elevate their fucking *class status* and start buying into how sexy and liberating it could be to *just be with each other*. But sadly those Black queers are as stuck social-climbing as I'm stuck licking up whatever stale white crumbs I can get my hands on which is why now is a great time to explain to you that *every* time you drunkenly ask me if I'm attracted to you because I'm a man and you're a man, I get infuriated not by how ignorant that question is, but by how much it actually bothers me to know that I probably *am* too fat and too Black and too ugly and too feminine to be a nigga you would even *theoretically* wanna dick down if you were gay and not my blood. Which is just how starved for Black affirmation and affection I am. And why I don't feel one iota of *Black-boy-joy-equality-whatever-the-fuck-it-is* anywhere in my body ever. Which is nobody's fault but my own for never asking for what I need or being accountable for my own bullshit I know, but just the same, worth saying out loud at least once. And that, in a nutshell, is "my personal life."

(Silence.)

THOUGHT 5: Son, what do you actually want from me?

USHER: I want you to like my writing. My music. This show. I want you to care about my complexity.

THOUGHT 5: Well, I *don't* like your writing, your music, or this show. And I don't give a rat's *ass* about your complexity and the sooner you get that through your hard-ass li'l' head, the easier it'll be. For all of us. Okay? Love you. Now. Sarabi, you hongry?

THOUGHT 4: Mufasa, it's all right. Calm—

THOUGHT 5: DON'T TELL ME TO CALM DOWN! YOU HEARD WHAT HE SAID—

THOUGHT 4: MUFASA, HE DON'T KNOW WHAT HE'S SAY—

THOUGHT 5: WHAT DID I DO TO DESERVE THIS? I DON'T DESERVE THIS!

THOUGHT 4: MUFASA!

USHER: JUST LET HIM GO!

THOUGHT 4: WHY DO YOU HATE US?

USHER: I DON'T HATE YOU.

THOUGHT 4: GETTIN' UP IN FRONT O' THE WORLD AND SHOWIN' EVERYBODY HOW MUCH YOU HATE US!

USHER: MOM, I DON'T HATE YOU! I DON'T HATE YOU!

THOUGHT 4: THEN WHY WOULD YOU WRITE ABOUT US LIKE THIS?!?

USHER: BECAUSE I LOVE YOU!!!

PRECIOUS LITTLE DREAM/AIDS IS GOD'S PUNISHMENT

THOUGHT 4: You don't love me! If you loved me, you wouldn't made your daddy run outta here with tears in his eyes! If you loved me, you woulda found you a church home up there in New York! If you loved me, you woulda brought me home a daughter-in-law and a grandbaby by now! If you loved me, you'd be able to fly me around the world like Tyler Perry!

THOUGHTS 5 AND 6:
HER PRECIOUS LITTLE DREAM

THOUGHT 4: But oh no, you off writin' about life!

THOUGHTS 5 AND 6:
CAME TUMBLING DOWN

THOUGHT 4: Never mind Doodoo Bank Student Loans calling my house lookin' for yo' Black butt!

THOUGHTS 1 AND 3:
>AND AFTER ALL THE TIME SHE SPENT BUILDING
>IT UP

THOUGHT 4: Just lallygaggin' up there in New York ain't half doin' NUTHIN'!

THOUGHT 2:
>AND AFTER ALL OF THE THINGS THAT SHE'S
>BEEN THROUGH

THOUGHT 4: Prob'ly out there dressin' up and pretending like you a *white woman*!

THOUGHT 3:
>YOU COME ALONG AND CRUSH IT

THOUGHT 4: Talkin' 'bout you "want a Black man"! Tuh!

THOUGHT 5:
>IN THE PALM OF YOUR HAND

THOUGHT 4: Like a real Black man would wanna kiss *you*!

THOUGHT 2:
>YOU COME ALONG AND FLUSH IT

THOUGHT 4: The Bible says the homosexsh'alities is worse than MURDER!

THOUGHT 6:
>DOWN

THOUGHT 4:
MY PRECIOUS LITTLE DREAM

USHER: It never ends with you!

THOUGHT 4:
OF A LITTLE BOY

USHER: Shampoo, rinse, repeat, repeat, repeat!

GOD, AFTER ALL THIS TIME WHY CAN'T YOU GIVE
IT UP?

THOUGHT 4: Oh no. You not gon' turn this on me. I *know* I'm
a good mama.

USHER:
'CAUSE IF YOU KNEW ALL THE THINGS THAT
I'VE BEEN THROUGH

THOUGHT 4: They had to *cut me open* to get you. Did you know
that? I bled and bled and they pulled yo' Black butt outta
my stomach.

USHER:
YOU'D RUE THE WAYS YOU ATTACKED ME

THOUGHT 4: Yo' Aint Hattie said the homosexsh'alities was just
a phase.

USHER:
YOU'D RUE THE WAYS WE FOUGHT

THOUGHT 4: But you twenty-six years old and *still* kissin' on men.

USHER:

> YOU'D RUN UNTIL YOU TRACKED ME

THOUGHT 4: Why couldn't you just be the dorter I always
wanted?!?

USHER:

> DOWN

THOUGHT 4: I'ma tell you why. It's 'cause you selfish!

USHER:

I'm not selfish! You always say that and all you're doing is deflecting from your own failures! You're fucking MADDENING! You and your FUCKING UNSOPHISTICATED, UNEDUCATED, UNCULTURED GOSPEL PLAY *FANTASY WORLD*!!!

THOUGHT 4:

NAHP! NAHP! NAHP! I don't be always sayin' *nothin*'! I be tellin' the truth! You don't care about *nobody* but ch'*own*self!

USHER:

> MAMA I CAN'T SUCK YOUR TITTIES AGAIN
> I CAN'T CRAWL BACK UP INSIDE YOUR WOMB

THOUGHT 4: Yo' nasty little mouth!

USHER:

> YOU WONDER WHY IT'S LIKE A GRAVEYARD
> IN YOUR LIVING ROOM

THOUGHT 4: And all I can do is cry!

USHER:

YOU WANNA CRY, MAMA? GO RIGHT AHEAD!

THOUGHT 4: My steps are growing short on this earth, my son!

USHER:

BUT I WON'T CRY, MAMA! 'CAUSE I'M NOT DEAD

THOUGHT 4: And one day you won't have me at all!

USHER:

AND YOU'RE NOT DEAD . . .

THOUGHT 4: Then you'll be *all* alone . . .

USHER:

TIME JUST HAS THIS WAY OF TEARING DOWN
   THE DREAMS WE THINK WE LIVE IN
SPINNING WHEELS IN MOTOR TOWN
SO EFFED-UP AND SO RUN-DOWN
AN OVERBLOWN YET FALSE DISPLAY
JUST LIKE IN A GOSPEL PLAY

(The set begins to shift into a gospel play. Thought 4 watches.)

THOUGHTS 1–3, 5–6:

WHO THE FUCK IS YOU, NIGGUH?
WHO THE FUCK IS YOU?
WHO? WHO? WHO?

(Usher transforms into The Color Purple *version of himself.)*

USHER: All mah life ah had to *fight*. 'Cause ah was smaht and 'cause ah was a Negro and 'cause ah was all off into the homosexsh'alities? But ah 'members dat day you *seed* me, Sarabi. When you seed me becomin' somebody you love but somebody you ain't like 'cause folk don't like nobody too proud or too free. But little did you know; ah wadn't neither one.

THOUGHTS 1–3, 5–6:
    WHO THE FUCK IS YOU, NIGGUH?
    WHO THE FUCK IS YOU?
    WHO? WHO? WHO?

(Usher transforms into The Real Housewives *version of himself.)*

USHER: Haaaaay, Sarabi, hay gurl. It's your son-slash-dorter you always wanted. I ain't want nuthin'. I was jes' callin' to talk to my mom 'n' ast you if you 'member the time we all went to Aint Hattie's seventieth birthday party 'n' dat airhead Marion got up to talk about what a good Sunday school teacher Aint Hattie was and how if there was one thing you learnt in her classes it was that she did *not* like gay people. 'N' everybody laughed 'n' clapped 'cause it was funny but also 'cause they ain't like gay people either? And I'm sitting there like "'member me?"

ALL THOUGHTS:
    WHO THE FUCK IS YOU, NIGGUH?
    WHO THE FUCK IS YOU?

(Usher transforms into the megachurch-pastor version of himself. A casket rises.)

USHER: Suhsta Sarabi, the Lord put it on my heart to sing this selection in honor of Brother Darnell who was an abomination just like me. And I can't help but reflect on the ways that I have lived a life without passion in fear of you and your husband's words to me that if I ever acted on my lust for another man, that I would meet the same fate as Darnell lying in that there box. And those words have kept me HIV-free but absolutely terrified because I realized then and there that the only thing worse than dying of AIDS would be living with it and hearing the people you loved say, "I told you so, I told you so, I told you so." Can I get a witness out there, Choir?

THOUGHTS 1–3, 5–6: Yaaaaaaaasssssssssss!!!!!!!!!!!!!!!

USHER: And so *on* today . . . as we prepare to bury yet another un-HBO-specialed, un-Oscar-So-White-award-winning, ab*Normal-Heart*ed, un-*Angel-in-America*n Black queer in the ground, it's very important that we remember what Gawd's word, your word, Tyler's word, and every fuckin' body else's word tells us:

AIDS IS GOD'S PUNISHMENT

THOUGHT 5: Sing your song, brutha, sing your song.

USHER:
FOR THE MAN WHO AIN'T LIVIN' RIGHT

THOUGHT 1 *(Points to her queer nephew in the audience)*: You hear that, Curtis?

USHER:
AIDS IS GOD'S PUNISHMENT

THOUGHT 6: I love the Lord, he heard my cry and pitied *every* groan, Pastuh!

USHER:

FOR HE WHO SINS IN THE NIGHT

THOUGHT 2: Let 'em know, let 'em know, let 'em KNOW!

USHER:

A-A-A-AIDS IS GOD'S PUNISHMENT
BUT ALL DARKNESS ALL DARKNESS
ALL DARKNESS ALL DARKNESS
COMES TO LIGHT

THOUGHT 3: Speak on it!

USHER:

HE GONNA KNOCK THEM DICKS UP OUT YO'
    MOUTH
AND THEN

And here's what I *like* about Him!

THEE THEE THEE THEE THEE THEE THEE THEE
    THEE THEE THEE
THEE HE SHALL SMITE! 'CAUSE

USHER, THOUGHTS 1 AND 2:
AIDS IS GOD'S PUNISHMENT!

USHER:
Sing, Sopranos! *Testify*
for all o' God's chirren!

THOUGHTS 1 AND 2:
YASSSSSSSSSSS!!!!!!

AIDS IS GOD'S PUNISHMENT!

USHER *(Continued)*:
Everybody in the building
clap wit' me on the 2 and 3
wit' my *altoooooos!*

(The altos lead everyone in clapping)

I HAD A PRAYIN'
GRANDMUTHA!

THOUGHTS 3 AND 4:
AIDS IS GOD'S PUNISHMENT!
YASSSSSSSSSSS!!!!!!

C'mon, Tenors—
AIDS!!!!!!!!

AIDS IS GOD'S PUNISHMENT!

These men are delivert!
I don't care what Sista
Mattie been sayin'
about 'em!

THOUGHTS 5 AND 6:
AIDS IS GOD'S PUNISHMENT!
YASSSSSSSSSSS!!!!!!

AIDS IS GOD'S PUNISHMENT!

Let's put it all together now
and fill the house of the
Lord with praise!

THOUGHTS 1–3, 5–6:
AIDS IS GOD'S PUNISHMENT!

Feels just like fire sat up
in mah bones!

YASSSSSSSSSSS!!!!!!
AIDS IS GOD'S PUNISHMENT!

The spirit of the Lord
is in this temple!

Can you feel it, Church?

AIDS IS GOD'S PUNISHMENT!
YASSSSSSSSSSS!!!!!!
AIDS IS GOD'S PUNISHMENT!

Can you feel it, Church?

AIDS IS GOD'S PUNISHMENT!
YASSSSSSSSSSS!!!!!!

Make me feel it, Church!
Make me feel God's
punishment! Parts!

AIDS IS GOD'S PUNISHMENT!

USHER *(Continued)*:
GOD IS GONNA DO IT!

> THOUGHTS 1 AND 2:
> AIDS!
> THOUGHTS 3 AND 4:
> AIDS!
> THOUGHTS 5 AND 6:
> AIDS!

GOD IS GONNA DO IT!

> THOUGHTS 1 AND 2:
> AIDS!

SORES ALL ON YO'
BODY AND YO' MOUF
AND IN YA BUTT!

> THOUGHTS 3 AND 4:
> AIDS!
> THOUGHTS 5 AND 6:
> AIDS!
> THOUGHTS 1 AND 2:
> AIDS!

RASHES AND
PNEUMONIA! THEN
YOU LAY STILL!

> THOUGHTS 3 AND 4:
> AIDS!
> THOUGHTS 5 AND 6:
> AIDS!
> THOUGHTS 1 AND 2:
> AIDS!

AIDS IS GOD'S
    PUNISHMENT WHEN
    YOU FUCK AGAINST
    GOD'S WILL!

> THOUGHTS 3 AND 4:
> AIDS!

USHER *(Continued)*:	THOUGHTS 5 AND 6:
AIDS IS GOD'S PUNISHMENT WHEN YOU FUCK AGAINST GOD'S WILL!	AIDS!
	THOUGHTS 1 AND 2:
	AIDS!
AIDS IS GOD'S PUNISHMENT WHEN YOU FUCK AGAINST GOD'S WILL!	THOUGHTS 3 AND 4: AIDS!
	THOUGHTS 5 AND 6: AIDS!
	THOUGHTS 1 AND 2:
AIDS IS GOD'S PUNISHMENT WHEN YOU FUCK AGAINST GOD'S WILL!	AIDS!
	THOUGHTS 3 AND 4: AIDS!
	THOUGHTS 5 AND 6: AIDS!

ALL THOUGHTS:
AIDS IS GOD'S PUNISHMENT . . .

(Cool down: Usher as Pastor is exhausted. He walks around the church at his own pace but still ministering, more quiet and reflective now.)

USHER: Let's bring it on down, Church, let's bring it on down.

ALL THOUGHTS:
AIDS IS GOD'S PUNISHMENT . . .

USHER: Can somebody get me a cup o' wawtuh please?

(One of the Thoughts brings him a cup of water.)

ALL THOUGHTS:
   AIDS IS GOD'S PUNISHMENT . . .

   (The choir continues to sing "AIDS is God's punishment" on loop over the following:)

USHER: Thank you, Jesus. Come on, Church, 'n' rock with me now.
   (Swaying side to side, hugging himself) What a mighty, mighty Gawd we serve that he would bring us together to celebrate the death and destruction of another one of us filthy fags. Filthy little sissy Darnell who I visited in the hospital. Darnell who found out he was sick ten years ago and decided to let Gawd's punishment ravish his body rather than get himself HIV medication because even *that* little faggot knew that the wages of sin was death. Sister Mattie, would you give us Second Peter, Chapter 2, Verse 12 please?
THOUGHT 1 *(Projecting to the back of the church; couldn't be prouder of herself for both being called on and for knowing the verse)*: "But *these*, as natural brute *beasts*, MADE to be taken and destroyed, speak *evil* of the things that they understand not; and shall *utterly* perish in their own corruption."
USHER: Amen. Brute beasts. Animals. That's what we faggots and trannies are. Filthy. Fistin' each other all the way up to the elbow and the shoulder. Shit and blood in our bed-sheets. Runnin' 'round wit' half our assho' hangin' out and *come* drippin' down our legs. Church, y'all don't hear me. Curtis, you don't hear me. 'Cause not only do you gotta prayin' grandmutha you got a talkin' auntie and, boy, if I had my way I'd put you and all the rest of us faggots in a cage 'n' set us on fire. Especially us *nigguhs*. 'Cause *we* the ones that let the white man trick us into thinking we free to do what we wont with our bodies and not what

Gawd wonts. And *we* the ones that let these airheaded Black Twitter faggots and these dat-blasted Black tranny "blahgers" and "vlahgers" trick us into thinking that AIDS is about "state violence" and "white su-premacy" and "het-er-o-pa-tri-ar-chy" and "po-ver-ty" and "secrets" and "shame" and "silence" and "stigma" like we ain't got a King James Bible that *clearly* tells us to not put a dick in our mouf. But we are so blessed. For the Gawd we serve rained down *burning* sulfur on Sodom and Gomorrah. "'Til there was *nothing* but dense smoke rising from the land like a furnace." Genesis 19:27, Amen. And *now* he's raining down this *beautiful* disease to show just how much he hates us pitiful Black fags. And he gon' *keep* executin' us 'til we learn who is the Lord thy Gawd. YAS-*SUH*! Sister Mattie take us on home!

(Thought 1 takes over. Usher tries to glory in what he's made, but it is an obviously false glory.)

ALL THOUGHTS *(Except 4)*:
AIDS IS GOD'S PUNISHMENT! YASSSSSSSSSSS!!!!!!

THOUGHT 1: Gawd is not mocked, Church!
THOUGHT 4: USHER! PLEASE STOP THIS!

ALL THOUGHTS *(Except 4)*:
AIDS IS GOD'S PUNISHMENT!

THOUGHT 1: For them lezzzzbians too! I see you, Tanisha! Ha *ha*!
THOUGHT 4: STOP SINGING THAT MUSIC!

ALL THOUGHTS *(Except 4, a cappella)*:
AIDS IS GOD'S PUNISHMENT!

(The choir of Thoughts exits. Thought 4 takes a shaken Usher into her arms. Silence.)

USHER: You wanted a gospel play and this is the only way I knew how to do it.

THOUGHT 4: Oh, Usher. You are loved, you are loved, you are loved. And you are so talented! I had no idea you was struggling like this. And *poor, poor Darnell*. It really brought a tear to my eye. 'Cause if he hadn't been out there living that gay lifestyle, he would still be here just like the pastor in the play said.

(Usher looks up.)

But at least we still got you. And we want you to go *up* and not *down* so we gon' get you on the right track if it's the last thing we do. And it might just be. Especially since yo' niece's *airheaded mama* done threaten to firebomb my house if I don't make yo' brutha marry her.

THOUGHT 1: GRAAAAANDMAAAAA! I GOTTA JOOOOB FOR YOUUUUUUUU!

THOUGHT 4: Heh-heh-heh. You hear that? Nala "has a joooob for me." Well, let me call you back. But don't worry. As long as you is sincere in your desire to *change your life for the better*, we go'n' work this gay abomination thang *out*.

(Usher pulls away.)

THOUGHT 6: GRAAAAANDMAAAA! IT PISSES GOD OFF IF YOU WALK BY A *COLOR PURPLE* QUOTE AND DON'T NOTICE IT!!!!!

THOUGHT 4: Heh-heh-heh-heh-heh. Okay.

(A pause. Thinks about it, brightens up:)

Ooh. Here's one: "This life be over soon. Heaven last always."

THOUGHT 2: GRANDMA, "YOU OUGHTA BASH MIS-TER HEAD IN AND WORRY ABOUT HEAVEN LATUH!"

THOUGHT 4: "I may be Black, I may be ugly, but I'm here!" Heh-heh-heh-heh-heh . . .

(Stops laughing suddenly; silence.)

Are you really sure this is how you want to end it, Usher? Just what are you trying to prove?

USHER: I'm just trying to show . . . what it's like.

THOUGHT 4: What what's like?

USHER: Life. Real life.

THOUGHT 4: And making a hateful Tyler Perry–style gospel play is real life?

USHER: It wasn't hateful. It was complex.

THOUGHT 4: Fine. But is this *really* what real life is like?

(Silence.)

USHER: Maybe not but that's what it *feels* like. To me. Sometimes. Or what it felt like. Especially when I was seventeen and telling my family who I was for the first time.

THOUGHT 4: Fair enough. But you're twenty-six now. So what's next?

USHER: I dunno. I truly don't know.

THOUGHT 4: Well, okay but *(Indicates the audience)* these people are not gonna wait for you forever. They wanna know when they can go home. We wanna know too.

(Thought 4 exits.)

MEMORY SONG

USHER: Okay, okay; I got this, I got this. So if Usher's sense
of self is just a bunch of meaningless symbols in his brain
moving from one level of abstraction to another but end-
ing up back where they started then his perceptions of
Mom and Dad and everything else are realities that will
never change until *he* changes. So what are the implica-
tions of that for Usher? And what does that make me?

FIVE FOOT FOUR
HIGH SCHOOL GYM
SNEAKING A CUPCAKE
THESE ARE MY MEMORIES
THESE ARE MY MEMORIES
SHOOTING HOOPS
OFF THE RIM
SLOW ON THE UPTAKE
THESE ARE MY MEMORIES
THESE ARE MY MEMORIES

AFTER GYM
THE LOCKER ROOM
MY EYES PHOTOGRAPHING
NAKED ME
MEASURES IN AT FOUR AND A HALF INCHES
THESE ARE MY MEMORIES
THESE ARE MY MEMORIES

OF ONE LONE BLACK GAY BOY I KNEW WHO
    CHOSE TO TURN HIS BACK ON THE LORD
ONE LONE BLACK GAY BOY I KNEW WHO
    CHOSE TO TURN HIS BACK ON THE LORD

GUILT AND SHAME
JESUS' NAME
CHURCH EVERY SUNDAY
THESE ARE MY MEMORIES
THESE ARE MY MEMORIES
EAT HIS BODY
DRINK HIS BLOOD
COMMUNION BUFFET
THESE ARE MY MEMORIES
SWEET SOUR MEMORIES

AFTER CHURCH
WE'RE DRIVING HOME
TO RADIO CRACKLE
JAZZ MUZAK
OR MOTOWN BLUES
AND SKIN IS A SHACKLE
FOR ONE LONE BLACK GAY BOY I KNEW WHO
    CHOSE TO TURN HIS BACK ON THE LORD
ONE LONE BLACK GAY BOY I KNEW WHO
    CHOSE TO TURN HIS BACK ON THE LORD

THESE ARE MY MEMORIES
SWEET SOUR MEMORIES
THIS IS MY HISTORY
THIS IS MY MYSTERY

USHER, THOUGHTS 2–6:
    HMM . . . HMM . . .

USHER:
    MOM IS NAPPING ON THE COUCH AND DAD CUTS
        THE GRASS WHILE
    I WATCH TV ALL DAY LONG: *YOUNG AND THE
        RESTLESS*

LIKE ONE LONE BLACK GAY BOY I KNEW WHO
    CHOSE TO TURN HIS BACK ON THE LORD
ONE LONE BLACK GAY BOY I KNEW WHO
    CHOSE TO TURN HIS BACK ON THE LORD

DAD IS DRUNK AND ON THE COUCH WHILE MOM
    EATS A PORK CHOP
"DAILY BREAD" MILL DAILY TREADMILL WON'T
    EVER STOP
ONE LONE BLACK GAY BOY I KNEW WHO
    CHOSE TO TURN HIS BACK ON THE LORD
ONE LONE BLACK GAY BOY I KNEW WHO
    CHOSE TO TURN HIS BACK ON THE LORD

I AM LYING ON THE COUCH I DREAM THAT I'M
    FLYING
FLAPPING BOTH MY WINGS SO HARD TO KEEP ME
    FROM DYING
WITH A CROWN OF GODFORSAKEN THORNS ON
    MY HEAD

LIKE ALL THOSE BLACK GAY BOYS I KNEW WHO
    CHOSE TO GO ON BACK TO THE LORD . . .

THOUGHTS 2–6:
    LIKE ALL THOSE BLACK GAY BOYS YOU KNEW WHO
    CHOSE TO GO ON BACK TO THE LORD

USHER:
    ALL THOSE BLACK GAY BOYS I KNEW WHO
    CHOSE TO GO ON BACK TO THE LORD . . .

THOUGHTS 2–6:
    ALL THOSE BLACK GAY BOYS YOU KNEW WHO
    CHOSE TO GO ON BACK TO THE LORD

USHER:

> ALL THOSE BLACK GAY BOYS I KNEW WHO
> CHOSE TO GO ON BACK TO THE LORD . . .

THOUGHTS 2–6:

> ALL THOSE BLACK GAY BOYS YOU KNEW WHO
> CHOSE TO GO ON BACK TO THE LORD

USHER:

> AND ONE LONE BLACK GAY BOY I KNEW WHO
> CHOSE TO TURN HIS BACK ON THE LORD . . .

THOUGHTS 2–6:

> CHOSE TO TURN HIS BACK ON . . .
> CHOSE TO TURN HIS BACK ON THE LORD . . .

USHER:

> INSTEAD . . .

(Thought 1 enters and joins the other Thoughts.
> *Usher turns his back to us as in the beginning. He rings his*
chimes.)

So that's it?

(Rings his chimes.)

That's really how the show ends?

(Rings his chimes.)

He just turns his back?

(Rings his chimes.)

But is he okay? Does he make it? Does he get the change he wants so badly?

(Rings his chimes.)

And if he does get the change he wants, what is he facing now?

(Rings his chimes.)

Or does he not change and it just starts all over again?

(Rings his chimes.)

Or maybe . . .

(Rings his chimes.)

The audience can't go home . . .

A STRANGE LOOP (FINALE)

USHER: Until he faces himself?
THOUGHT 1: Faces himself?
THOUGHT 2: Faces himself?
THOUGHTS 1–3: Faces himself?
THOUGHTS 1-4: Faces himself?
THOUGHTS 1–5: Faces himself?
ALL THOUGHTS: Faces himself? Faces himself?

(Usher turns to the audience and faces himself.)

USHER:

I AM THIS STORY'S WRITER
I'M BARELY SCRAPING BY
I WAKE UP EVERY MORNING
I TELL MYSELF TO TRY

I SAY NO COMPROMISES
I CLAIM TO HAVE A PLAN
WHEN I AM NOTHING MORE THAN
AN ANGSTY GAY, BLACK MAN
WHO LOOKS INTO THE MIRROR
DESPITE THE GRIEF IT BRINGS
WHO HEARS THESE SLOPPY ESSES
BETRAY HIM AS HE SINGS

SOMETIMES I FEEL SO UGLY
SOMETIMES I FEEL SO SMART
SOME PEOPLE STAND TOGETHER
ME, WELL, I STAND APART

SHOULD I GIVE UP ON HOPING
MY POINT OF VIEW WILL SHIFT
AND LET THIS AGONY
JUST BE MY GREATEST GIFT?

BUT IF THAT IS THE SECRET
THAT MAKES LIKE ZERO SENSE
I'LL NEVER CHANGE FOREVER
IF I STAY ON THE FENCE

WITH DOUBTS I LET DEFINE ME
AND LUST I CAN'T EXPRESS
AND PAIN I KEEP AVOIDING
AND RAGE THAT I REPRESS

I SHOULD STOP OVERTHINKING
AND DO THE THING THAT'S TOUGH
UNLEASH MY HUNGRY LION
'CAUSE DOROTHY'S HAD ENOUGH
OF TOXIC TYLER PERRY
AND WHITE GAY MALE TYRANNY
AND MY SECRET INNER WHITE GIRL
THOUGH SHE IS DEAR TO ME

BUT WOULD THAT BE SUFFICIENT?
OR WOULD THAT BE A SHAM?
'CAUSE EVEN WITH THOSE ACTIONS
I'M STUCK WITH WHO I AM

SOMEONE WHOSE SELF-PERCEPTION
IS BASED UPON A LIE
SOMEONE WHOSE ONLY PROBLEM
IS WITH THE PRONOUN "I"
MAYBE I DON'T NEED CHANGING
MAYBE I SHOULD REGROUP
'CAUSE CHANGE IS JUST AN ILLUSION

THOUGHTS 1 AND 2:
JUST AN ILLUSION . . .

THOUGHTS 3–6:
JUST AN ILLUSION . . .

USHER:
AND "I" IS JUST AN ILLUSION

THOUGHTS 1 AND 2:
JUST AN ILLUSION . . .

THOUGHTS 3–6:
>   JUST AN ILLUSION . . .

USHER *(Faces his Thoughts)*:
>   IF THOUGHTS ARE JUST AN ILLUSION

THOUGHTS 1 AND 2:
>   JUST AN ILLUSION . . .

THOUGHTS 3–6:
>   JUST AN ILLUSION . . .

USHER:
>   THEN WHAT A STRANGE

ALL THOUGHTS:
>   STRANGE . . . STRANGE . . .

USHER:
>   STRANGE . . . LOOP . . .

>   *(Blackout.)*

MICHAEL R. JACKSON's *A Strange Loop*, the 2020 Pulitzer Prize– and New York Drama Critics' Circle Award–winning musical, was called "a full-on laparoscopy of the heart, soul, and loins" and a "gutsy, jubilantly anguished musical with infectious melodies" by Ben Brantley of the *New York Times*; and "exhilarating and wickedly funny" by Sara Holdren of *New York*. In the *New Yorker*, Vinson Cunningham wrote: "To watch this show is to enter, by some urgent, bawdy magic, an ecstatic and infinitely more colorful version of the famous surreal lithograph by M. C. Escher: the hand that lifts from the page, becoming almost real, then draws another hand, which returns the favor." As a songwriter, Michael has seen his work performed everywhere from Joe's Pub to National Alliance

BEOWULF SHEEHAN

for Musical Theatre (NAMT). In addition to *A Strange Loop*, he also wrote book, music, and lyrics for *White Girl in Danger*; and lyrics and book for the musical adaptation of the 2007 horror film *Teeth*, with composer and co-book-writer Anna K. Jacobs. Awards and associations include: the Pulitzer Prize, a New Professional Theatre Festival Award, a Jonathan Larson Grant, a Lincoln Center Emerging Artist Award, an ASCAP Foundation Harold Adamson Award, a Whiting Award, the Helen Merrill Award for Playwriting, a New York Drama Critics' Circle Award, an Outer Critics Circle Award, a Drama Desk Award, an Obie Award, an Antonyo Award, the Hull-Warriner Award, the Frederick Loewe Award, and a Dramatist Guild Fellowship. He is an alum of Page 73's Interstate 73 Writers Group. He has commissions from Grove Entertainment and Barbara Whitman Productions, and LCT3. He is a member of the Dramatists Guild Council. *A Strange Loop* received its world premiere in 2019 at Playwrights Horizons in association with Page 73 Productions.

*Theatre Communications Group would like to offer
our special thanks to the board and staff of
Playwrights Horizons for their generous support of
this publication of* A Strange Loop
*by Michael R. Jackson, in recognition of
outgoing Artistic Director Tim Sanford*

PLAYWRIGHTS HORIZONS is a writer's theater dedicated to the support and development of contemporary American playwrights, composers, and lyricists, and to the production of their new work.

———

THEATRE COMMUNICATIONS GROUP's mission is to lead for a just and thriving theatre ecology. Through its Core Values of Activism, Artistry, Diversity, and Global Citizenship, TCG advances a better world for theatre and a better world because of theatre. TCG Books is the largest independent trade publisher of dramatic literature in North America, with 18 Pulitzer Prizes for Best Play on its book list. The book program commits to the life-long career of its playwrights, keeping all of their plays in print. TCG Books' authors also include: Annie Baker, Nilo Cruz, Jackie Sibblies Drury, Larissa FastHorse, Athol Fugard, Jeremy O. Harris, Quiara Alegría Hudes, David Henry Hwang, Branden Jacobs-Jenkins, The Kilroys, Tony Kushner, Young Jean Lee, Tracy Letts, Lynn Nottage, Dael Orlandersmith, Suzan-Lori Parks, Sarah Ruhl, Stephen Sondheim, Paula Vogel, Anne Washburn, and August Wilson, among many others.

Support TCG's work in the theatre field by becoming a member or donor: www.tcg.org

tcg